A Most Dangerous Profession

A Most Dangerous Profession

Why the Pastoral Ministry Is Hazardous to Your Soul

Eric C. Sorenson

RESOURCE *Publications* · Eugene, Oregon

A MOST DANGEROUS PROFESSION
Why the Pastoral Ministry Is Hazardous to Your Soul

Copyright © 2011 Eric C. Sorenson. All rights reserved. Except for brief quotations in critical publications or reviews, no part of this book may be reproduced in any manner without prior written permission from the publisher. Write: Permissions, Wipf and Stock Publishers, 199 W. 8th Ave., Suite 3, Eugene, OR 97401.

Resource Publications
An Imprint of Wipf and Stock Publishers
199 W. 8th Ave., Suite 3
Eugene, OR 97401

www.wipfandstock.com

ISBN 13: 978-1-60899-527-1

Manufactured in the U.S.A.

This study is dedicated to my wife, Karyn, whose unwavering commitment to Christ, encouragement, and wisdom, have helped sustain me during two decades of pastoral ministry together.

Contents

Preface ix
Introduction 1

Part One: Three Early Church Fathers

Chapter 1   Gregory of Nazianzus   7

Chapter 2   John Chrysostom   16

Chapter 3   Gregory I   25

Part Two: Some English Pastoral Theologians

Chapter 4   A Thousand Years Later   37

Chapter 5   George Herbert   46

Chapter 6   Richard Baxter   51

Chapter 7   Gilbert Burnet   65

Chapter 8   George Bull   77

Chapter 9   William Paley   83

Part Three: Looking for Solutions

Chapter 10   Remedies from the Pastoral Theologians   93

Chapter 11   Retirement   100

Chapter 12   Self-Knowledge   103

Chapter 13   Study   107

Conclusion   110

Bibliography   119

Preface

MY DESIRE IN THIS book is to join in on the ongoing conversation over pastoral health, but from a pastoral and spiritual theology perspective. The thrust of the current dialog revolves around the damage that pastoral ministry can inflict upon the pastor's emotional, relational, and physical health. This risk, it is often suggested, must be addressed by a healthier lifestyle that amounts to diligent self-care. This study is intended to focus on the spiritual hazards that accompany pastoral ministry, and argues that the church's historic voice is a unified warning that the pastoral ministry involves risks to the soul of the practitioner, risks with profound implications.

This study began after noticing repeated warnings in some of the early Christian literature concerning these spiritual hazards and sacred risks. After a careful analysis of Gregory of Nazianzus's Third Oration, John Chrysostom's *Six Books on the Priesthood*, and Gregory the Great's *Book of Pastoral Rule*, a surprisingly unified concern was noticed. Even more surprising, this same concern was found to reemerge in the writings of certain English pastoral theologians, along with clear advice on how to face these hazards.

By means of comparing the first writers to the second writers, it is seen that the latter were dependent upon the former, and thus, together they provide the contemporary church with important and timeless warnings about the spiritual risks that accompany pastoral ministry. Fortunately, along with the alarm sounded over spiritual risks, these latter writers also provide unified and relevant guidelines for overcoming these concerns.

That being stated, I want to acknowledge the fact that since the time our subjects wrote their great contributions, more and more women have entered into the folds of professional church ministry. Since the writers

I have studied knew of nothing but male clergy, I have faced a bit of a challenge in that my intention here is to be inclusive of all God's servants. Thus, I have done my best to employ both male and female pronouns throughout this book in reference to pastors, while trying to maintain the integrity of the writers' personal situations. To the degree that this book falls short of that endeavor, I take full responsibility, but implore the reader's grace.

This work is written to all pastors, those who care for pastors, and those who train pastors. It constitutes my feeble attempt to join the pastor-support team, a team consisting of denominational leaders, counselors, spiritual directors, teachers, family members, prayer warriors, and seminary officials. It is my sincere hope that a renewed awareness of this ancient and timeless wisdom will provide strength for today's pastor, thereby reaping eternal benefits in the lives of those in their care, and bringing greater glory to the Lord of the church.

This project would not have come to fruition without the invaluable guidance and support of many individuals. I would like to acknowledge my indebtedness to Dr. James Bradley, Geoffrey W. Bromiley Professor of Church History at Fuller Theological Seminary, theological mentor, and tremendous source of information and support. His love for the English pastoral writers, in particular, watered the seed of my curiosity, and developed into this present book. I would also like to thank the many people God has allowed me to shepherd over the twenty-five years since I entered into this "art of arts and science of sciences" (Gregory of Nazianzus). So much of the present work reflects personal lessons learned while ministering among you. Furthermore, I am indebted to the faculty and staff of Pacific Islands University and Evangelical Seminary in Guam, where I have been given the privilege of serving as seminary dean. Finally, to my wife, Karyn, and our children, Teyler, Christian, Katie, and Noelle, I owe much gratitude for understanding and accepting my need to hide away and complete a study that I hope will benefit Christ's church. To God alone be all the glory.

Introduction

No one who has engaged in pastoral ministry would dispute the notion that the role is unique; in fact, it could be argued that there is no job like it. Usually, there are no fixed hours, so most pastors work notoriously long ones. It concerns itself primarily with the intangible part of being human, so success is difficult to measure. It is accompanied by a smattering of enormously different responsibilities, yet no training for some of them. The sad fact is that the expectations placed on pastors are so high that it is not uncommon to run into a burned-out ex-pastor. Thus, much attention has recently been given to the phenomena of pastoral burnout. Kirk Byron Jones summarizes the concern: "One of the main reasons for pastoral stress and burnout is the vast number of tasks that pastors are asked to perform, and perform well. The pastor is expected to fulfill a variety of responsibilities and to possess knowledge about a vast array of concerns related to the church and to the community at large."[1] Out of this concern, there has emerged a common consensus: Pastors must give greater attention to their own personal health. Again, Jones: "Clergy members must learn to confess personal overload and hurry as threats to our bodies (self and family), to the body of Christ, and to the body politic. We must confess insufficient self-care as a subtle but lethal expression of personal and social violence."[2] Jones goes on to describe the self-violence pastors often commit, the "spirit of ecclesial competition"[3] pastors experience, and those aspects necessary to overcome these pressures, such as pacing one's life, finding stillness, and discovering balance.

---

1. Kirk Byron Jones, *Rest in the Storm: Self-Care Strategies for Clergy and Other Caregivers* (Valley Forge: Judson Press, 2001), 1.
2. Ibid., 8.
3. Ibid., 18.

Not to invalidate these burnout concerns, there is, nevertheless, something that seems to be missing from much of the contemporary literature. While there is great attention given to the practical, or functional, aspect of ministry, there is less emphasis placed on the spiritual and theological side. Thus, contemporary concerns over pastoral health usually identify the practicalities of daily ministry as the root of so much ill, while so often failing to give attention to issues related to either pastoral or spiritual theology. This oversight leaves out a whole set of foundational factors that, at the very least, would result in presenting a richer array of resources for those struggling in ministry.

To address this missing ingredient, we will look back to the history of pastoral theology that repeatedly emphasized both the core spiritual nature of the pastor's work and its deep theological significance. Thus, the thrust of the literature we will survey is theological rather than functional, and spiritual rather than practical. To be sure, these older writers gave a great deal of attention (some may conclude *too* much attention) to the demands inherent in ministry, but by in large, these demands are not of the functional variety, but of the theological and spiritual variety. Further, instead of focusing on the practical dangers we label "burnout" and "depletion," these writers spotlight the tremendous spiritual and theological hazards that come with the call; they raise questions that we scarcely consider. Is there an intrinsic threat to the pastor's own spiritual self that accompanies the demands that come with the office? Is it possible that a pastor's concern over another's soul can be so overwhelming that it blinds the pastor to his or her own spiritual condition? Do pastors face greater temptations than those that rage against the average Christian? The witness of the older pastoral theologians leaves no doubt: Attached to pastoral ministry is a set of specific spiritual dangers that threaten to ruin the soul of the one called to carry out that ministry. Without question, in the minds of the earlier pastoral theologians, there are hazards inherent in the task itself, and these are spiritual and theological by nature.

I was first alerted to this theme by reading John Chrysostom, which led me back to Gregory of Nazianzus, and then forward to Gregory the Great. So, we begin by considering these three, among the early church's greatest figures, who shared the belief that the pastoral ministry (for them, *priestly* ministry) is a dangerous place for one's soul. Beginning with Gregory of Nazianzus's Third Oration, also called *Apologeticus De Fuga*, moving to John Chrysostom's *Six Books on the Priesthood*, also known as *De Sacerdotio*, we will finally consider Gregory the Great's seventh century *Book of Pastoral Rule*, originally titled *Liber Regulae Pastoralis*. Emerging out of their individual defenses for their decisions to flee the call to ministry and refuse ordination (to the papacy in the case of Gregory the Great), these church leaders underscore a series of personal warnings about the hazards one encounters in the pursuit of pastoral ministry. In other words, the spiritual dangers inherent in ministry forge the core reason these writers rejected the call to priestly office to begin with. There are certainly differences between the three, as we will notice, but "they all take their origins in their authors' unwillingness to accept ecclesiastical office."[4] Together, these documents constitute a unique sub-genre of Christian literature united by their desire to explain their dramatic actions, which they accomplish with a remarkable unity of voice.

Since each document is intended to explain a specific incident, we must begin with an overview of the author's life story, followed by the often fascinating details that lie behind the document, before we overview the literature itself. Allowing the authors to speak for themselves as much as possible, it will then become clear that at the heart of their defenses is a common concern about the unique spiritual demands of the pastoral office and the spiritual hazards that accompany those demands. Though writing about unique personal decisions based upon different motivations, all three of these writers agree that the demands of pastoral ministry are great, and the potential for spiritual ruin that accompany the office are many. It is those demands and hazards that are the primary subject of this first section.

Building on the concerns articulated by the three ancient writers, we then turn our attention to a renewed concern over the same issues expressed by certain English pastors who lived, ministered, and wrote in the seventeenth and eighteenth centuries. As will be more carefully explained in the introduction to the second part, it is clear that these later writers were directly influenced by, and perhaps dependent upon, the earlier ones. Although these Early Modern English writers were not motivated by the same need to offer a defense for fleeing the ministry, they nevertheless express the same basic concerns about the spiritual risks that come with pastoral work.

---

4. Graham Neville, introduction to *Six Books on the Priesthood*, by St. John Chrysostom (New York: St. Vladimir's Seminary Press, 2002), 20.

In the second part, then, we focus on some comments contained in George Herbert's highly influential *Country Parson*, we give detailed attention to Richard Baxter's *Reformed Pastor*, and Gilbert Burnet's *A Discourse of the Pastoral Care*. These same concerns for the spiritual vitality of pastors, accompanied by warnings about the dangers inherent in their work, will then be seen through the contributions of several others in various sermons preached during this period. Here we look at a significant sermon by George Bull who directly addresses this concern, and another by the famous William Paley, who offers a unique angle to the concern at hand.

Valuable though a book of spiritual warnings might be, it would be an injustice to ignore the plethora of advice that also emerges from these writers. Focusing again on the practical nature of the English thinkers, the final section highlights some of the most common appeals made to the pastoral community as to what must be done to overcome these constant spiritual hazards. By incorporating the advice of other authors from this period, we draw some final conclusions by observing advice that ranges from developing good study habits to the desperate need for self-knowledge.

My singular desire is to offer another important piece to the growing body of literature concerning pastoral health. Different than focusing on the risks of an unhealthy lifestyle, this contribution highlights the spiritual risks that always accompany the call to pastoral ministry. If there is any one thing that these diverse writers should reveal to us, it is that these spiritual hazards are part of the very fabric of the work pastors do. Thus, a pastor can be religious about scheduling in rest and making sure he or she works at a healthy pace, but live completely ignorant of the spiritual landmines that accompany the office.

I believe it is time for the contemporary church to revisit some of these forbearers in order to seek the wisdom of the ages "and ask for the ancient paths, where the good way lies" (Jeremiah 6:16, *NRSV*). Their esteem of the pastoral office should cause us to compare our own views, if we are willing to face the discrepancy we might find. Their deep theological understanding of the nature of the work pastors do, along with their profound doctrine of the pervasive nature of sin, brings to light a new way of looking at this high-risk adventure called pastoral ministry. Fortunately, their advice as to what to do about these hazards is timeless.

PART ONE

Three Early Church Fathers

Chapter 1

Gregory of Nazianzus

This is the extremest of dangers in the eyes of everyone.

WE MEET TWO GREGORYS in our study, but they must not be confused, for their lives were separated by three centuries, hundreds of miles, and two distinct languages. However, as we will also see in the case of John Chrysostom, both Gregorys shared a common fear of the pastoral office.

Gregory of Nazianzus was raised on the family estate in the city of Nazianzus, near Cappadocia, in what is today, Turkey. Born about 330, he was nurtured by a godly mother and his bishop father. He was educated at Caesarea where he met Basil, who, along with Basil's brother, Gregory of Nyssa, would later become known by the historic church as the Cappadocian Fathers. Sometime around 350, Gregory and Basil traveled to Athens to seek further education until Gregory returned to Nazianzus in 358 to teach rhetoric and help his aging father. Meanwhile, Basil had established a small hermitage in Pontus which Gregory frequented. It was in Nazianzus where the event unfolded that gave rise to his *Apologeticus*.

Here, probably on Christmas Day in either 361 or 362, his father forced priestly ordination on him.[1] By Easter, Gregory seems to have been over his initial hard feelings, and had returned to join his father in ministry. Even though his friend, Basil, now metropolitan of Cappadocia,

---

1. Andrew Purves, *Pastoral Theology in the Classical Tradition* (Louisville: Westminster John Knox, 2001), 11.

insisted that Gregory become bishop of the small village of Sasima, he refused, and continued his work in Nazianzus until his father's death in 374. Hoping to retire to a life of contemplation, he was summoned to service by the faithful in Constantinople in 379. There he energetically served the Church of the Resurrection and "made a significant contribution to the final establishment of the orthodox faith."[2] After the council of Constantinople, Gregory went back to his home in Nazianzus to serve the church. Finally, in 384, he retired to his family's estate, where he died somewhere between 389 and 391.

Referred to as "beyond doubt one of the greatest orators of Christian antiquity,"[3] Gregory's written trail is marked with a series of recorded orations. His most famous are *Five Theological Orations*, delivered to defend the teaching of Nicea. A second group, orations twenty and thirty-two, Quasten lumps together because of their common attempt to denounce his hearers for fancying argument and controversy.[4] An apologetic group of orations, along with a group of panegyrical orations are rounded out by the largest group, his occasional orations. The most famous of these occasional orations is the second, *Apologeticus de Fuga*, "which amounts to a complete treatise on the nature and responsibilities of the priestly office."[5] Beyond the rich collection of Gregory's orations, there are some four hundred poems extant and more than 240 letters.

APOLOGETICUS DE FUGA

The selection of writings from the first Gregory, John Chrysostom, and Pope Gregory, are joined by a common thread of the authors' resistance to accepting pastoral office. All three writings under consideration make this clear. The occasion of Gregory of Nazianzus' Second Oration, then, is stated in his subtitle: "In defense of his flight to Pontus." We can say with some certainty that the contents of this oration refer to the events of Christmas, 361 or 362, when his father forced ordination upon his son. This event caused his "flight" to the Iris River in Pontus, the habitation of

---

2. G. L. Carey, "Gregory of Nazianzus" in *The New International Dictionary of the Christian Church*, ed. J. D. Douglas (Grand Rapids: Zondervan, 1978), 435.

3. Johannes Quasten, *Patrology*, 3 vols. (Utrecht: Spectrum Publishers, 1963), 3:236.

4. Ibid., 3.242.

5. Ibid., 3.237.

his trusted friend, Basil. Apparently charged with cowardice, this oration is his attempt to explain the reasons for his disappearance.[6]

The importance of Gregory's defense, however, is not limited to its historical interest. The Second Oration is also an insightful fourth-century depiction of the nature of the pastor's work. With characteristic beauty, Gregory writes, "But the scope of our art is to provide the soul with wings, to rescue it from the world and give it to God, and to watch over that which is in His image, if it abides, to take it by the hand, if it is in danger, to restore it, if ruined, to make Christ to dwell in the heart by the Spirit: and, in short, to deify, and bestow heavenly bliss upon, one who belongs to the heavenly host" (2.23). The priest's call is a high and lofty one, meant to bring a soul to God. No wonder, foreshadowing Gregory the Great, he calls the priesthood "the art of arts and science of sciences" (2.16).

Beyond the lofty call, however, this great church thinker presents a powerful picture of the intense demands of the priestly office, along with the spiritual hazards attendant to it: "This [priestly ministry] is of all things most to be feared, this is the extremest [sic] of dangers in the eyes of everyone who understands the magnitude of success, the utter ruin of failure" (2.99). In short, as Quasten puts it, "He describes at great length the character and responsibilities of the sacerdotal office, in order to justify himself for first fleeing from its burdens and then returning to submit to them."[7] The bulk of Gregory's work then seeks to spell this out. His argument flows in keeping with a masterful rhetorician, organized, and rich in language and imagery.

He begins the defense of his "flight" by offering four reasons for it. First, there was the simple suddenness of it all. He complains that he was "thrust into the midst of a life of turmoil by an arbitrary act of oppression" (2.6). Second, what he really wanted from life was isolation, "escaping from the flesh and the world, collected within myself, having no further connection than was absolutely necessary with human affairs" (2.7). Gregory, writes Quasten, was weak and of an extremely sensitive nature,[8] which would, of course, make the interpersonal demands of ministry almost overbearing. Third, Gregory faced the problem of association. He was ashamed of the others who served in the same profession, "Pitiable as

---

6. Gregory of Nazianzus, *Apologeticus de Fuga* (A. D. 362?), 2.2. Hereafter, all citations will be in-text.

7. Ibid., 3.237.

8. Ibid., 236.

regards piety, and unfortunate in their dignity" (2.8). In Gregory's estimation, never before "has there ever been such an abundance, as now exists among Christians, of disgrace and abuses of this kind" (2.8).

Lastly, Gregory offers a reason for rejecting pastoral office that then launches him into the next section of his oration. His final reason for rejecting office is put plainly: "I did not, nor do I now, think myself qualified to rule a flock or herd, or to have authority over the souls of men" (2.9). His profound reaction against his ordination was partly due to his deep sense of being unqualified for the lofty call of priestly ministry. Sensing the apparent need to elaborate on this, the final cause of his refusal, he moves on to offer another list of four. Now, four reasons for his feeling disqualified.

First, he does not meet the high standard of pastoral ministry because anyone taking on the great task of pastoral ministry must be pure, "Since the injury which extends to many is greater than that which is confined to a single individual" (2.10). His deficiency in moral purity is not just limited to staining his own soul; it extends to the souls of others. After all, "Nothing is so easy as to become evil" (2.11).

This implicit confession of moral impurity leads him to his second disqualification. He fails to meet the high standard because in virtue he is lacking. "He must not only wipe out the traces of vice from his soul, but also inscribe better ones, so as to outstrip men further in virtue than he is superior to them in dignity" (2.14). Obviously, Gregory's ideas of what was needed to qualify one for the office required not only an absence of evil, but an abundance of good.

It could be suggested that his third objection does not stand on its own because it seems to thread all of his disqualifications together like some sort of summary; nevertheless, Gregory himself sees it as a separate disqualification. He simply could not accept the office because the priestly ministry is "the art of arts" (2.16). Perhaps due to the potent analogy between the priest caring for souls and the physician caring for bodies, Gregory expands on this third disqualification from section 16 through section 34. Here Gregory is at his rhetorical best: "Any one may recognize this, by comparing the work of the physician of souls with the treatment of the body; and noticing that, laborious as the latter is, ours is more laborious, and of more consequence, from the nature of its subject matter, the power of its science, and the object of its exercise. The one labors about bodies, and perishable failing matter . . . The other is concerned with the soul, which comes from God and is divine, and partakes of the heavenly

Gregory of Nazianzus 11

nobility, and presses on to it, even if it be bound to an inferior nature" (2.16, 17). To Gregory, there is simply no comparison between the call of the two professions: The priest's is higher than the physician's.

The final reason he offers for his being disqualified from the priestly office is connected to what he calls "the first of our duties" (2.35), which is the preaching and teaching of the Word of God. The call is exacting because the thought of being in doctrinal error was to Gregory, a horrible sin. Therefore, by virtue of the elevated status of the call to preach and teach, he finds himself incapable of taking office. Gregory devotes the next several sections to demonstrating from Scripture how the call to pastoral ministry is extremely serious and demanding. From Paul, to the prophets, to Jesus himself, the standards are nearly unbearable (2.51–77).

In an apparent jump back to his claim that contemporary priests were bringing shame on the church (cf. 2.8), Gregory now elaborates on this theme, making the claim that priests are shameless, ungodly, and that the name of Christ is blasphemed by them (2.78–86). Only now does Gregory begin to wind down and move back to the initial question prompting this Second Oration. In short, the ministry is dangerous! To accept this call "is of all things most to be feared, this is the extremest of dangers in the eyes of everyone who understands the magnitude of success, the utter ruin of failure" (2.99).

The foregoing then begs a question: Why did Gregory return to this high and dangerous call? He concludes his oration by offering three reasons. At the top of the list is his longing to be back with his brothers and sisters he so deeply missed (2.102). Secondly, he felt a profound duty to return to care for his aging parents (2.103). Finally, he returned, as he puts it, because "I remembered the days of old, and, recurring to one of the ancient histories, drew counsel for myself therefrom" (2.104). The rest of his treatise expands on this "ancient history", which amounts to a recollection of the famous story of the prophet Jonah. The proverbial bottom line is that Gregory returned to the pastorate out of sheer obedience. He did not want to, but obedience compelled him.

DEMANDS AND HAZARDS

Flowing from the preceding overview of Gregory's oration are several ideas that speak specifically to our present concern. In fact, the priestly ministry is marked by tremendous spiritual demands, and even hazards, that are intrinsic to it since the purpose of the ministry is "to make Christ to dwell in the heart by the Spirit" (2.23). Gregory sees this clearly and articulates it with force in *de Fuga*.

To begin with, the priestly office is an extremely high calling. As we have seen, in Gregory's words, "The guiding of man, the most variable and manifold of creatures, seems to me in very deed to be the art of arts and science of sciences" (2.16). In comparison with the office of the physician, the demands on the pastor are far greater, for treating his or her subject is more varied and complex than the physician is often charged to treat. Gregory recognizes that this challenge is beyond his reach. This "branch of philosophy is, however, too high for me, the commission to guide and govern souls — and before I have rightly learned to submit to a shepherd, or have had my soul duly cleansed, the charge of caring for a flock" (2.78). This is the essence of why our three subjects rejected their ordination. For various reasons, the call was higher than they felt capable of reaching. In fact, all of the demands and hazards attendant to the pastoral office are due to its lofty nature.

Second, in Gregory's mind, the pastor/priest must be free from evil and superlative in goodness. In short, the pastor must be pure. It is inconceivable to Gregory that a dirty vessel would be effective in bringing cleanliness to another dirty vessel. The first vessel itself must be clean. "A man must himself be cleansed, before cleansing others: himself become wise, that he may make others wise; become light, and then give light: draw near to God, and so bring others near; be hallowed, then hallow them; be possessed of hands to lead others by the hand, of wisdom to give advice" (2.71). Impurity is a horrible disease for the pastor because it hinders the transmission of the message like a clogged pipe impedes the free flow of water. Since we are absolutely dependent upon the Holy Spirit by "whom alone we are able to perceive, to expound or to embrace, the truth in regard to God" (2.39), we must be pure and receptive vessels. So purity allows for the work of the Spirit, which is integral to our perceiving truth: "For the pure alone can grasp Him Who is pure and of the same disposition as himself" (2.39).

Finally, it is no surprise that Gregory stresses the necessity of being strong to serve in the priesthood. Among other reasons for this necessary strength, the pastor must be aware that the people under his or her care can adversely affect the purity of their pastor if the pastor is not strong enough to resist. Gregory is satisfied in describing the church in terms of constant warfare amongst itself, to the degree that even the priests are caught up in it (2.81). In this section of the oration, he is addressing the overall problem with the current state of the priesthood, while trying to make the case that both the people and the priests are in an equally bad state (2.82). So Gregory writes: "Nor indeed is there any distinction between the state of the people and that of the priesthood: but it seems to me to be a simple fulfillment of the ancient curse, 'As with the people so with the priest'" (2.82). This is yet another impetus for Gregory to retire to a life of isolation; in short, he is too weak:

> For I own that I am too weak for this warfare, and therefore turned my back, hiding my face in the rout, and sat solitary, because I was filled with bitterness and sought to be silent, understanding that it is an evil time, that the beloved had kicked, that we were become backsliding children, who are the luxuriant vine, the true vine, all fruitful, all beautiful, springing up splendidly with showers from on high. For the diadem of beauty, the signet of glory, the crown of magnificence has been changed for me into shame; and if anyone, in face of these things, is daring and courageous, he has my blessing on his daring and courage. (2.90)

If the demands of the priesthood are not enough to intimidate the best pastoral candidates, in the course of his Second Oration, Gregory also identifies its spiritual hazards, hazards to the pastor's personal life, and hazards that threaten the souls of those entrusted to the pastor. The greatest personal spiritual threat is that of judgment, a concern repeated by all of three early church writers, and not a few English pastoral theologians. "For it is to be feared that we shall have to hear these words concerning those who have been entrusted to us: I will require their souls at your hands; and, Because ye have rejected me, and not been leaders and rulers of my people, I also will reject you, that I should not be king over you; and, As ye refused to hearken to My voice, and turned a stubborn back, and were disobedient, so shall it be when ye call upon Me, and I will not regard nor give ear to your prayer" (2.113). In what is certainly the most intimidating threat, Gregory recognizes the hard statements of Scripture and sees no way around them: those who fail in their ministry will fail to pass judgment in the eyes of the God of the universe, "For one in high estate, if he fail to make further progress and to disseminate virtue still more widely, and contents himself with slight results, incurs punishment" (2.101). So Andrew Purves: "Small wonder he was terrified at the responsibility."[9]

9. Purves, 19.

The reality of divine judgment is not the only personal spiritual hazard one encounters in ministry, because along with the responsibility to distribute the Word, there comes the risk of teaching false doctrine. Thus, far from seeing preaching as a great opportunity for ministry, Gregory is intimidated by it: "Now this involves a very great risk to those who are charged with the illumination of others" (2.36). Almost ironically, from this great Cappadocian Father, this potent force in the promulgation of orthodox doctrine, there surfaces the threat that there is inherent spiritual risk in teaching Christian truth simply because the priest may get it wrong. Noting great doctrines like the Trinity, the Resurrection, the Incarnation, and others, Gregory asserts that it would be a spiritual tragedy for the pastor to misrepresent the truth of God. To "speak unrighteousness" (2.41) is a sin that amounts to no less than "treason to the truth" (2.40).

Naturally, such treason would also result in hazards for those under the care of an inept shepherd. Inculcating wrong doctrine not only results in the teacher's judgment, it brings ruin to the student, which goes directly against the purpose of the priest's ministry to heal those who have been ruined (cf. 2.23). This ruin not only comes from error in theology, it comes through spiritual illness on the part of the priest. This is dangerous to the degree that "the wider his rule, the greater evil he will be. Since the injury which extends to many is greater than that which is confined to a single individual" (2.10). Using some of the Old Testament's emphasis on the contagion of sin, Gregory warns the pastor not to be guilty of the same. We must make sure, at all costs, that we do not "undertake to heal others while ourselves are full of sores" (2.13).

We allow Gregory to draw a conclusion by means of the florid prose so characteristic of his writing:

> Let others sail for merchandise, I used to say, and cross the wide oceans, and constantly contend with winds and waves, to gain great wealth, if so it should chance, and run great risks in their eagerness for sailing and merchandise; but, for my part, I greatly prefer to stay ashore and plough a short but pleasant furrow, saluting at a respectful distance the sea and its gains, to live as best I can upon a poor and scanty store of barley-bread, and drag my life along in safety and calm, rather than expose myself to so long and great a risk for the sake of great gains (2.100).

In the end, we must agree with the judgment of Andrew Purves: "What Gregory has done, metaphorically speaking, is place a 'spiritual health warning' over every candidate for holy orders."[10] As we will now observe, Gregory is not the only one to issue such warnings; he was but the first.

---

10. Ibid., 26

Chapter 2

John Chrysostom

More billows toss the priest's soul than the gales which trouble the sea.

TREATING OUR SUBJECTS CHRONOLOGICALLY brings us to Saint John Chrysostom and his magisterial *On the Priesthood* (*De Sacerdotio*). Like Gregory, his predecessor in Constantinople, John rose to the apex of his power as bishop of that great city, but not without initially rejecting the call to the pastoral office. Also like Gregory, John left behind a kind of apology for his actions.

It helps to see John's life in four stages: his early years, his first years of ministry, his service as bishop, and the years of controversy. J. N. D. Kelly, in his authoritative biography of John, places his birth in Antioch in the year 349.[1] It appears that the family of John was rather well off. His father, Secundus, a senior civil servant, was not a Christian, and died while John was still an infant. His mother, Anthusa, however, was a devout Christian who exercised great influence on her son. Showing great intellectual promise from an early age, John studied the classical curriculum of his day and later sat under the famous philosopher Libanius. Attracted early on to Christian studies, John was baptized at twenty-three, "The pivotal moment of his life."[2] It took his childhood friend, Basil, however, to turn John's attention away from the allurement of the theatre to full devotion to

---

1. J. N. D. Kelly, *Golden Mouth* (Grand Rapids: Baker, 1995), 4.
2. Andrew Purves, *Pastoral Theology in the Classical Tradition* (Louisville: Westminster John Knox, 2001), 35.

the Christian life. Basil effectively convinced John to enter a life of solitude and meditation, but his mother would have none of it, which frustrated John's monastic ambitions. Thus, instead of leaving home, John turned the family residence into a kind of monastery where he lived a simple, ascetic life, marked by study and prayer. For three years he attended to the bishop and advanced as a reader while studying theology under the direction of Diodore of Tarsus. It was only after his mother's death that John finally found the opportunity to retreat to a life of solitude that he so long desired. By way of summary, his biographer, Palladius, wrote: "He then retired to a cave by himself, in his eagerness to hide himself from the world, and there spent twenty-four months, for the greater part of which he denied himself sleep, while he studied the covenants of Christ, the better to dispel ignorance. Two years spent without lying down by night or day deadened his gastric organs, and the functions of his kidneys were impaired by the cold. As he could not doctor himself, he returned to the haven of the Church."[3]

His return to the city Kelly dates at 378, at which time John realized that the damage to his health prevented him from living such an austere life.[4] Upon his return, John was immediately ordained a deacon. Finally, about five years later, in 386, he was ordained to the priesthood. His fame was forever secured after he was given the special duty of preaching in the principal church of Antioch. For twelve years "he discharged this office with such zeal, ability and success that he established forever his title as the greatest of Christian pulpit orators," earning him the nick-name "Chrysostom" ("Golden-mouthed").[5]

His promotion to bishop of the great city of Constantinople in October of 397 probably came as a surprise to him, but it is debated whether or not he welcomed it.[6] Either way, partly because of John's personality, he soon found himself in trouble with the city's royalty. As Chadwick explains, "John was ascetic, aloof, energetic, and outspoken to the point of indiscretion, especially when he became excited in the pulpit."[7]

---

3. Cited in Johannes Quasten, *Patrology*, 3 vols. (Utrecht: Spectrum Publishers, 1963), 3.425.

4. Kelly, 36.

5. Quasten, 425.

6. Purves hints that John welcomed the bishopric (36), while Quasten claims John "did not show any willingness to accept" the office (3.425).

7. Henry Chadwick, *The Early Church* (New York: Dorset Press, 1986), 188.

Andrew Purves is helpful in outlining the next twists and turns that eventually lead to John's death.[8] First, John traveled to Ephesus in 401 and deposed several bishops there, charging them with simony. During his absence, the empress, Eudoxia, organized a movement to depose the bishop partly because of her rejecting his attempts at moral reform. At John's return, true to his character, he preached a sermon in which he made an obvious connection between the empress and the wicked biblical character, Jezebel. The empress got the implication, and the war was on.

Second, John found himself involved in defending fifty Origenist monks who Theophilus, bishop of Alexandria, had expelled. Theophilus then sailed to Constantinople and, at the famous "Synod of the Oak" in 403, banished John from the city. Upon the citizens' outcry, and a deadly earthquake the day following his banishment, the officials reversed their decision.

The final straw fell when John responded to a statue the empress had erected of herself in front of the great church, *Hagia Sophia*. Likening her to the biblical Herodias demanding the head of John the Baptist, this John pushed Eudoxia to convince her husband to banish the bishop. In 404, John was deposed. After being banished again in 407, this time even further away, he died feeble, old, and sick.

"Among the Greek Fathers, none has left so extensive a literary legacy as Chrysostom."[9] Besides the significance of Chrysostom's theological contributions, the sheer output of his writings is astonishing. The largest segment of those writings is the vast array of sermons. Quasten categorizes these sermons into exegetical homilies, dogmatic and polemical sermons, moral discourses, sermons for liturgical feasts, and panegyrics.[10] Besides the sermons, Chrysostom penned a significant number of treatises on various topics, including the monastic life, virginity, the education of children, and suffering. One of these great treatises is *De Sacerdotio*. Rounding out the collection of John's writings are his letters, of which 236 are extant. Throughout these writings, John is known as a champion of orthodoxy, being clearly of the Antiochene school of exegesis, which scorned typology in preference to taking the text in its plain

---

8. Purves, 37, 38.
9. Quasten, 3.429.
10. Ibid.

historical-grammatical sense. For instance, his sermons on Genesis total sixty-seven, each of which consists of verse-by-verse exegesis.

ON THE PRIESTHOOD: DE SACERDOTIO

Like his predecessor Gregory, John penned this work out of a desire to explain his own flight from ordination. The feel of the book is different, however, for it consists of a reported dialogue between himself and his boyhood friend, Basil. The historical veracity of this account will be considered later; for now, it will suffice to note the intimidating portrait of priestly ministry Chrysostom paints.

The circumstances behind the book are reflected in a comment Basil makes toward the end of it.[11] The reason he came to his friend John was to find out what excuse he had for running from the call to priestly ordination. The whole of the book is a description of the conditions surrounding his decision, a decision, he explains, that started with a rumor. "We [John and Basil] were to be promoted to the dignity of the priesthood . . . I was overcome with fear and bewilderment: with fear, that I should be seized against my will, and with bewilderment, as I tried again and again to guess what had induced the men concerned to form such a plan for me. I examined myself and discovered nothing that deserved such an honor (1.6)."

The unique nature of Chrysostom's story, however, is found in the deceit he hoisted on his friend. Apparently, in a clever attempt to mislead his pursuers, John agreed to meet Basil and succumb to ordination with him, but when the hour arrived and Basil was ordained, his friend, John, was nowhere to be found! Part of his defense to Basil was his conviction that while he was unfit for such an office, Basil was not, and the church would be strengthened with Basil as a priest (1.6).

This is at least what appears to motivate Chrysostom's *Six Books*. However, as Purves points out, John's primary intention was to instruct the church on priestly reform and the responsibilities and difficulties of the pastoral office.[12] Only secondarily was this treaties intended as an apologetic. Regardless of what was John's original motivation, the genre of the literature is an apology that amounts to a wealth of information regarding the pastor's call.

---

11. John Chrysostom, *de Sacerdotio* (AD 391), 6.13. Hereafter, all references will be cited in-text.

12. Purves, 42.

All of this leads to the often debated question regarding the veracity of the circumstances behind the *Six Books*. Purves, for one, suggests that the document may not be based in fact, but may have been fabricated as a rhetorical device to admonish and warn priests.[13] In other words, his flight from ordination was not the primary motive for his writing in the first place. The basis for this suggestion is that the acknowledged authorities on John's life do not mention such an episode, the existence of Basil is questionable, and the document is laid out in a rhetorical style that does not demand historical veracity. However, J. N. D. Kelley reacts to these suggestions and offers direct refutations to each one.[14] Agreeing with Kelly, historian Andrea Sterk concludes that recent historiography "has reestablished the underlying historicity of his autobiographical allusions."[15]

It is the timing of this incident in John's life that raises the most substantial question. Part of the debate here revolves around whether John rejected the call to the priesthood or to the episcopate. It is not clear whether the reference in 1.6 is to the priesthood, as the text literally reads, or the episcopate, since it is the latter that becomes the focus of his attention as the document unfolds. If the former is in view, the events of the book took place in 386. If the latter, the events transpired in 398. According to Kelly, probably the correct reading in 1.6 is "priesthood."[16] The case for it being a reference to his priestly ordination in 386 is further supported by other dates in John's life. It is probable that he makes reference to his desire to write *De Sacerdotio* in a homily preached undoubtedly in 388. We also know that St. Jerome refers to having read it in 393. Since it must have taken some time for it to reach Jerome, it is safe to conclude that *Six Books* was penned in about 390 or 391, several years before his elevation to the episcopate.[17]

Besides the debates that revolve around occasion and dates, a reading of John's work makes his theme rather clear: he rejected the call to the priestly office because the demands and responsibilities of the office were too high for him to possibly reach. "His real theme is the supremacy of the pastoral ministry and the exacting demands it makes upon those

13. Ibid., 36.
14. Kelly, 27.
15. Andrea Sterk, *Renouncing the World Yet Leading the Church: The Monk-Bishop Is Late Antiquity* (Cambridge: Harvard University Press, 2004), 149.
16. Kelly, 26.
17. A detailed look at the possible dates can be traced in Kelly, 25–26, 55, and 83.

who exercise it."[18] The work does not just present a negative theme, for it also instructs priests in the carrying out of this high, yet difficult calling. So Quasten comments: "It shows forth how venerable and how difficult is the office of the priesthood, and it shows how to fulfill it as it ought to be fulfilled."[19]

The theme plays itself out logically as the first book gives its complete attention to an explanation of the events surrounding his initial rejection of ordination. Book 2 continues the argument, but begins to make some initial observations on the nature of priestly ministry, giving detailed attention to the shepherd and sheep metaphor. In book 3, John finishes defending his decision to avoid ordination, and begins to identify some of the specific difficulties and challenges of the ministry. Books 4 and 5 concern themselves with the great art of preaching. This high calling, which gets to the core of the nature of the ministry, takes an incredible moral, spiritual, and intellectual toll on the priest. The fifth book begins to highlight some of the particular temptations that are attached to the ministry of teaching and preaching. John's work comes to its conclusion with a consideration of the demands put on the bishop, especially the call to purity.

DEMANDS AND HAZARDS

As was the case with Gregory of Nazianzus, our consideration of John's opinion regarding the pastoral ministry encompasses both its spiritual demands and hazards. In the first place, it is difficult to overstate just how intensely John regards the demand for purity among the priesthood. "The priest, therefore, must be as pure as if he were standing in heaven itself, in the midst of those powers" (3.4). It could be argued that the demand for purity is the core of his apology to Basil. Much of book 6 takes up this demand. Because of its high calling, the urgency to die to sin and allow Christ to reign is much greater for the pastor than it is for other believers. In fact, "The priest's soul must be purer than the rays of the sun in order that the Holy Spirit may never leave him desolate" (6.1). Again: "The soul of the priest ought to blaze like a light illuminating the world" (6.4). In context, of course, John's argument is that his soul does not blaze, thus he

---

18. Graham Neville, *Six Books on the Priesthood* by John Chrysostom (New York: St. Vladimir's Seminary Press, 2002), 34.

19. Quasten, 3.459.

is disqualified from the pastoral call. Not even the monk, John argues, has such a demand put on him, for the pastor must dwell among earthly and mundane matters, yet remain detached from them. In short, the pastor must be blameless while living in an impure world.

The call on the priest's life is intimidating of course, because the work of the ministry has people's perfection as its goal. Similar to his predecessor's claim that the goal of the work of the priest is to present people faultless before God (*de Fuga*, 2.22), "The man who is entrusted with it [the Church] must train it to perfect health and incredible beauty" (4.2). "For this is the ultimate aim of their teaching: to lead their disciples, both by what they do and what they say, into the way of that blessed life which Christ commanded" (4.8). The rationale of John's thinking is obvious. If the priest's role is to lead people to perfection, then the priest's own life must be perfect. It is no surprise then, that John regularly repeats the desperate need for tremendous strength to avoid failing. "How much strength in himself and from above do you think he needs to avoid complete failure?" (3.6). From John's vantage point in *Six Books*, the answer is ominous.

It follows that along with the spiritual demands placed on the pastor, there come spiritual hazards. Although the precise meaning of his warning is not clarified, to John, entering the priesthood actually exposes one to the loss of one's own soul. In a daunting warning, John writes, "But anyone entrusted with men, the rational flock of Christ, risks a penalty not of money but of his own soul for the loss of the sheep" (2.2). A sentence earlier, John suggested that a literal shepherd may receive "pardon" (συγγνώμης) for losing a sheep to a wolf, but this will not be granted to the shepherd of souls who loses a spiritual sheep; in fact, he will be penalized. So in the larger context, John is juxtaposing the notion of being *pardoned* with the notion of being *penalized*. "Penalty" (ζημίαν) carries the notion of disadvantage, damage, or forfeit. Such a penalty the pastor incurs for this kind of loss is inflicted on his own soul. Since συγγνώμης carries the idea of a concession or indulgence, it appears that the penalty incurred is non-forgiveness. Apparently, to John's way of thinking, there is no forgiveness granted the pastor who loses his sheep. Commenting on John, Purves concludes: "The ministry is dangerous work for the soul."[20] However, there may be some consolation in John's use of the plural form

---

20. Purves, 52.

of "men" and "sheep" in that he could be suggesting that such punishment strikes one who loses *all* of one's sheep.

Beyond the threat of losing one's soul, John's greater emphasis is on the constant temptations that attack the spiritual health of the pastor. In John's imagery, they are "billows" that blow against the soul of the priest. "More billows toss the priest's soul than the gales which trouble the sea" (3.7). Throughout the pages of John's treatise, he identifies a great number of these temptations. First, he identifies vainglory (3.7). Here John confesses that even in his present state, without being ordained, he has to fight this temptation. He knows that those billows blow even harder on those who are ordained. He returns to this idea in his treatment of preaching and teaching in book 5. His conclusion: "So a preacher must train himself above all else to despise praise" (5.6).

Ambition appears in the list of John's concerns about temptation as well. "We must be thoroughly on our guard against ambition and examine ourselves carefully to prevent a spark of it from smoldering anywhere unseen" (3.2). It is those who are ambitious for the office who are easy prey for the work of the enemy. Purves identifies why: "Ambition is the doorway through which evil enters the spirit, for one will do anything to seize the object of desire."[21]

In the flow of book 3, John changes his metaphor for temptation from billows to beasts, and proceeds to list not a few of them. Anger, dejection, envy, strife, slanders, accusations, lying, and hypocrisy are matched by teaching to please, ignoble flattery, contempt for the poor, and servile fear. As if those various temptations are not enough, he goes on in 6.12 to list even more, including "the constant society of women." These temptations combine, John says, to "tear my soul in pieces" (6.12). As a result, he longs to remain where he is (withdrawn and alone) than to be engaged in priestly ministry where he "will be left with nothing but their snarl. So I stick to this cell. I am isolated, unsociable, inhospitable" (6.12).

In the end, John's tact seems to have worked, for if he represents Basil's response accurately, Basil is humbled. Speaking of the excuse he was supposed to bring to the superiors as to why John refused ordination, Basil writes, "I am not concerned now with the excuse I shall make to them for you, but with the excuse I shall make to God for myself and my own sins" (6.13). John's elaborate defense that articulated strongly the

---

21. Ibid., 53.

daunting nature of pastoral ministry had apparently succeeded in striking fear into the heart of his friend. Indeed, if John is right, Basil is not the only one who should be so stricken

CHAPTER 3

Gregory I

Lest in helping others he desert himself, lest in lifting up others he fall.

ARRIVING ON THE SCENE centuries after the first Gregory and John Chrysostom, Pope Gregory is revered as one of the key figures in the development of the history of the Church and its theology. Certainly, part of his fame is due to his being pope of Rome, but what makes his name stand out from other popes is that he was "one of the ablest men ever to occupy that position."[1]

Although Gregory led an extraordinary life, few details of his early years are known; thus, his childhood is subject to some debate. It appears that he was born in Rome about 540 to a family that was aristocratic and Christian. The emperor, Justinian, ruled from Constantinople while the battle for Rome raged against the Ostrogoths. When the Ostrogoth King, Totila, besieged Rome in 545, the city fell apart under the pressure and surrendered the next year. In his youth, Gregory lived in the midst of a Rome in ruins, a faded image of its former self, rife with disease, destruction, and internal chaos.

Before the year 573, Gregory was made governor of the city by emperor Justinian II. Later, attracted to the contemplative life of the monk, Gregory devoted his wealth to the founding of monasteries and still later gave himself to this life by joining the monastery of St. Andrew. After

---

1. Justo Gonzales, *The Story of Christianity*, vol. 1, *The Early Church to the Dawn of the Reformation* (San Francisco: HarperSanFrancisco, 1984), 1.244.

Pope Benedict made him a deacon, the next pope, Pelagius II, appointed Gregory ambassador to the court of Constantinople where he spent six years involved in controversies both political and theological. After his long and devoted service, the pope then relieved Gregory of his service and allowed him to return to his monastery where he was made abbot. At this point, Rome was again in a crisis. This time, the city was threatened by the Lombards. To make matters worse, in the midst of the chaos, a horrible epidemic broke out in the city, wreaking death and havoc. The present pope, with Gregory as his able assistant, cared for the hungry, buried the dead, and kept the city clean. Suddenly, as if to add to the chaos, Pelagius was himself stricken ill and died. It was completely contrary to Gregory's desire to fill the highest office in Christendom, but against his wishes, his fellow priests chose him.

Although he entered the esteemed office with great reluctance, Pope Gregory took on the role with tremendous energy. Despite being somewhat subject to the emperor, Gregory was the real force that stood against the Lombard invasion. Under his leadership, troops were raised, tribute paid, and peace established. In short, during his tenure in office, Gregory managed to keep Rome from being conquered. "He was the strongest man in Italy, and must have seemed to the Romans and to the Lombards alike far more a real sovereign than the distant and feeble Emperor."[2]

The pervasive nature of Gregory's rule is almost unparalleled in church history in that the primacy of the Bishop of Rome expanded under his notion that *all* Christians are subject to Peter, not just those in Rome. Although he did not claim universal authority,[3] he expanded his influence practically and earned the title "Gregory the Great." A part of this far-reaching influence was affected through Gregory's aggressive missionary campaign to England. This effort not only expanded the influence of the Christian faith to the British Isles, but initiated a close tie between England and the papacy.

Although the actual contribution of Gregory to Church music is debated because no contemporary references to it can be found, tradition ascribes the reformation of church music in that period to him. "Gregorian chants" are attributed to the Pope along with the development of Roman liturgy. His profound influence as a preacher though, is not de-

---

2. Williston Walker, *A History of the Christian Church* (Edinburgh: T. &. T Clark, 1918), 191.

3. Gonzales, 1.246.

bated. Apparently, Gregory had tremendous oratory skills and used those skills to further his purposes. For instance, his influence as a preacher can be witnessed in his writings, a tremendous number of which are homilies. Extant are forty homilies on the Gospels and twenty-two on Ezekiel. Even his famous, and lengthiest, *Book of Morals* is essentially a commentary on Job that played a major role in the discussion of ethics during the Middle Ages. It is the collection of his letters though, that compose the largest bulk of his written legacy. Fourteen books of correspondence, totaling 854 letters is an impressive output, considering the fact that this is surely not the entire corpus from a lifetime of letter writing.

THE BOOK OF PASTORAL RULE: LIBER REGULAE PASTORALIS

Apparently, the first subject that concerned Gregory as the new pope was the state of his clergy, for his first papal writing was *Liber Regulae Pastoralis*. Here it is important to remember the social and political state of Rome during Gregory's ascendancy to office. Rome was marked by pandemonium created through a vacuum of power; this disastrous situation was mirrored by the state of the priesthood. Thus, the document contains a plethora of instructions to clergy in carrying out their sacred ministries in the midst of a world in turmoil.

Very similar to the writings of both the earlier Gregory and John, Pope Gregory's document is a defense for having initially refused a holy call. Unlike the earlier two men who rejected a call to priestly ministry, in Gregory's case, the rejection was the refusal to take the highest office after the death of Pelagius II in February, 590. As we have noted, after Pelagius' death, Gregory was immediately elected to the office, which prompted him to go to work contesting his election. First, he fired off a letter to Emperor Maurice imploring him not to confirm his election. Thomas Oden suggests that for a period of time he went into hiding.[4] To his chagrin, he was confirmed six months later, whereupon the citizens and clergy of Rome carried him bodily to St. Peter's where he was formally consecrated on September 3, 590. "There is no doubt from subsequent letters that for the rest of his life he regretted his elevation. He truly wanted to remain a monk, a modest

---

4. Thomas Oden, *Care of Souls in the Classic Tradition* (Philadelphia: Fortress Press, 1984), 48.

director of souls, and a quiet contemplative."⁵ Despite his protestations and regrets, Gregory faithfully served his office fourteen years.

The *Regulae* itself begins as a response addressed to John, bishop of Ravenna, who had earlier sent Gregory a letter that reproved him for rejecting the office. The occasion then can be found in Gregory's own words: "With kind and humble intent thou reprovest me, dearest brother, for having wished by hiding myself to fly from the burdens of pastoral care; as to which, lest to some they should appear light, I express with my pen in the book before you all my own estimate of their heaviness, in order both that he who is free from them may not unwarily seek them, and that he who has so sought them may tremble for having got them."⁶

What follows this opening apology is a document of nearly unparalleled influence. Oden states that "Gregory's *Pastoral Care* is the most influential book in the history of the pastoral tradition."⁷ Such an assertion may be an overstatement when we consider that Gregory's *Regulae* is itself the product of influence. Clearly Gregory's predecessor in genre was John, and John's was Gregory of Nazianzus. In fact, since the resemblance of the stories behind this body of literature are so pronounced, their content overlaps, which may mitigate Oden's claim. Nevertheless, the significance of the document under consideration is great. So Purves notes that in the *Regulae*, "The patristic contribution to the classical tradition in pastoral theology came to its crowning achievement."⁸

Even though Gregory's presented occasion for writing was to defend his retreat from papal election, he also clearly intended to guide and shape the priests under his care through his *Regulae*. It is really, therefore, "an exposition on the duties and qualities of the bishops of the church."⁹ Like the two documents considered earlier, there are certainly reasons for the *Regulae* that go beyond it being an apology for his flight from sacred service. Some of these reasons are to be detected in the flow of Gregory's argument, which he outlines in his opening section: "For, as

---

5. Ibid.

6. Gregory the Great, *The Book of Pastoral Rule* (AD 590), 1.1. Subsequent citations will be in text.

7. Oden., 115.

8. Andrew Purves, *Pastoral Theology in the Classical Tradition* (Louisville: Westminster John Knox, 2001), 55.

9. Edmund Clouse, "Gregory I" in *The New International Dictionary of the Christian Church*, ed. J. D. Douglas (Grand Rapids: Zondervan, 1978), 432.

the necessity of things requires, we must especially consider after what manner everyone should come to supreme rule; and, duly arriving at it, after what manner he should live; and, living well, after what manner he should teach; and, teaching aright, with how great consideration every day he should become aware of his own infirmity (1)." *Regulae* is not simply autobiographical; it is also meant to be an exhortation.

So Gregory's influential work falls into four parts. Part one deals with the character necessary for the office, what Purves labels "the faithful pastor."[10] The second section details the expectations and demands placed upon the pastor. The third treats the kind of teaching that should be implemented in pastoral ministry. This leads, fourth, to a fascinating look at the uniquenesses of people under care and how those differences demand special pastoral approaches, something Oden calls "contextual pastoral counseling."[11] His final section treats the reality of the pastor's own infirmities, and how such realities demand self-care. Ironically, beyond just defending his decision to reject the papacy, Gregory's first written work embraces his call as chief pastor.

DEMANDS AND HAZARDS

Gregory's contribution is abundantly clear in stating that the demands of pastoral ministry are many and great. The whole first section of his book, which at first appears to be concerned with the skills required to succeed in ministry, is really about the character that is required to be successful. First, the pastor must practice what he (and, in contemporary church culture, "she") preaches.[12] This is clearly a warning based on Gregory's observation that verbal instruction fails to create change if the example of the instructor is out of sync with what he or she is teaching. "But to foul the same water with their feet is to corrupt the studies of holy meditation by evil living. And verily the sheep drink the water fouled by their feet, when any of those subject to them follow not the words which they hear, but only imitate the bad examples which they see (1.2)." Gregory picks up this observation and repeats it elsewhere: "For indeed the preacher drinks out

10. Purves, 63.

11. Oden, 73.

12. In order to reflect Gregory's historical setting in which only men were allowed the priestly role, I am referring to priests with the male pronoun. To honor our contemporary setting, where women also serve as priests and pastors, I am including the female pronoun in parenthesis.

of his own cistern, when, returning to his own heart, he first listens himself to what he has to say. He drinks the running waters of his own well, if he is watered by his own Word . . . For indeed it is right that he should himself drink first, and then flow upon others in preaching. (3.24)."

The issue is serious. Not only will the one who does not practice one's preaching be ineffectual in engendering change, but that person actually causes the ruin of the student since that pupil becomes exposed to the teacher's hypocrisy. He (or she) must indeed be careful in the ministry of pastoral care lest "he become the cause of ruin to his subordinates" (1.10) because of his failure to live what he or she preaches.

A second consideration is that the pastor must weigh his own sinfulness. Using a curious reference to Leviticus 21.17, in which God instructs Aaron that all priests must be without blemish, Gregory presents a message concerning the sinlessness demanded of the pastor. "Speak to Aaron and say: No one of your offspring throughout their generations who has a blemish may approach to offer the food of his God" (NRSV). In a creative use of metaphor, Gregory urges his readers to understand that those physical blemishes which prohibited priestly service, have spiritual counterparts. A blemished nose, for instance, refers to the one who lacks discernment. A blinded eye is like the one who cannot see the light of truth. The hunchback is the one who is weighed down by the weight of the world. Thus the pastor is served a warning: "Whosoever, therefore, is subjected to any one of these diseases is forbidden to offer loaves of bread to the Lord, lest in sooth he should be of no avail for expiating the sins of others, being one who is still ravaged by his own"(1.11). Patterns of sin and shortcoming in the service of God disqualify one from pastoral office.

Thirdly, to be a pastor requires effective preaching. In Gregory's mind, the pastor fails miserably unless he or she fulfills the preaching task. His or her failure to preach, in fact, incurs the wrath of the judge whose coming he is supposed to pronounce. Like a herald going ahead of an important visitor, so goes the preacher, and the preacher must not fail! "For the priest, when he goeth in or cometh out, dies if a sound is not heard from him, because he provokes the wrath of the hidden judge, if he goes without the sound of preaching" (2.4). Further, the failure to preach also causes the ruin of the one who needs to hear the preacher's message. "Let them consider therefore with what punishment they must be visited who, when souls are perishing from famine of the word, supply not the bread of grace which they have themselves received" (3.25). The preaching task is a great demand, not simply as a task, but as a spiritual calling since the preacher is answerable to God and the hearers suffer if it is neglected.

Fourth, there are also the weighty attributes of character that are necessary for the pastor to be a pleasing servant. Beyond the deficiencies suggested by way of metaphor in Leviticus 21, there are spiritual qualities demanded of the minister. Gregory mentions compassion and mercy, which are qualities that must be shown to everyone (2.5). He goes on to mention sympathy, loving kindness, and contemplation. Once again, though, Gregory is not just contented to present the call to Christ-like character in a positive manner, but ends with an ominous warning: "Their [good pastors'] open works indeed we see; but what remains to them behind in the hidden retribution of the strict judge we know not" (2.5). Even those outward behaviors could be deceiving, but the ultimate Judge knows all and sees all.

Finally, all of section 3 in Gregory's profound writing concerns itself with "contextual pastoral counseling." It is easy to get caught up in the details of Gregory's insights into the uniqueness of people and disregard the larger point. One of the demands of pastoral ministry is the ability to know the sheep well enough to treat each one differently. Whether the pastor is caring for those who bewail sin or those who do not, those who are married, or those who are not, those who are learned or those who are ignorant, each situation demands a different response. Indeed, Gregory's insight is amazing, and even prescient of today's psychological insights into pastoral care. It is also an equally profound demand placed upon the one who takes up holy orders.

Perhaps it is no surprise that like Gregory's predecessors in this genre of spiritual writing, he not only outlines the demands of ministry, but highlights the hazards that come with the role. Oden notes: "Gregory was convinced that the guidance of souls carried special hazards for the guide. There is the danger that one may become so engaged in another's struggle that one decreases in level-headed self-awareness."[13] In fact, this is the first area of Gregory's express concern: the neglect of one's own spiritual health. This can be seen in the final section where Gregory emphasizes the importance of avoiding pride and becoming puffed up in carrying out the pastoral ministry. Here, he makes a statement concerning the pastor's

13. Oden, 61.

spiritual health that extends beyond issues of pride: "But since often, when preaching is abundantly poured forth in fitting ways, the mind of the speaker is elevated in itself by a hidden delight in self-display, great care is needed that he may gnaw himself with the laceration of fear, lest he who recalls the diseases of others to health by remedies should himself swell through neglect of his own health; lest in helping others he desert himself, lest in lifting up others he fall (4)." The pastor must pay attention to his (or her) own spiritual health. So, everything that the pastor brings to care for the soul of another, must first be inwardly applied.

Pride is the second area that Gregory specifically highlights as a potential hazard to the soul of the pastor. The danger here comes from the occasional praise the pastor receives. There is a danger, so to speak, that the pastor will believe the adulation the crowd lavishes on him (or her). In a comparatively long section on the subject, the pope's wisdom shines in his analysis of the hazard of pride and its subsequent affects.

> His mind, seduced by what is offered in abundance from below, is lifted up above itself; and, while outwardly surrounded by unbounded favor, he loses his inward sense of truth; and, forgetful of himself, he scatters himself on the voices of other men, and believes himself to be such as outwardly he hears himself called rather than such as he ought inwardly to have judged himself to be. He looks down on those who are under him, nor does he acknowledge them as in the order of nature his equals; and those whom he has surpassed in the accident of power he believes himself to have transcended also in the merits of his life; he esteems himself wiser than all whom he sees himself to excel in power (2.6).

Pride enters into the pastor's soul like an irrepressible vine and works its way through the whole of his or her being. Again, the danger is that the soul of the pastor, "Forthwith seeks its own praise, and begins to arrogate to itself all the good which it has received for shewing forth the praise of the giver; it desires to spread abroad the glory of its own reputation, and busies itself to become known as one to be admired of all"(4). So Gregory states pointedly, "Therefore, in the heart humility should be maintained, and in action discipline" (2.6).

From pride, Gregory then surfaces a third problem inherent in a ministry geared to caring for others. There comes with this ministry the tendency to want to so please those one cares for, that such a desire supersedes the call to please God first. "Meanwhile it is also necessary for the ruler to keep wary watch, lest the lust of pleasing men assail him; lest, when he studiously penetrates the things that are within, and providently supplies the things that are without, he seeks to be beloved of those that are under him more than truth (2.8)." Calling this tendency a lust, he taps into the core issue at hand: The desire to please can become an all-consuming passion that outweighs the fundamental call to pronounce truth.

Finally, Gregory is pointed and unrelenting in his confidence that each pastor will be held accountable for the souls of the people. Like our two other subjects, his language is straight-forward and unmistakable. In his articulating the demand that priests be free from sin, he manages to slip in the following warning: "Wherefore it is necessary that they guard themselves so much the more cautiously from sin as by the bad things they do; they die not alone, *but are guilty of the souls of others*, which by their bad example they have destroyed" (3.4, italics mine).

So in Gregory's mind, the sin of the pastor brings ruin on those under care, and most significantly here, the pastor will be held accountable for the final state of souls under his or her care, even to the point of being pronounced guilty. Indeed, Gregory's God is a strict judge who takes the responsibility to pastor with utmost seriousness. Using especially strong language, Gregory urges pastors to "consider therefore with what punishment they must be visited who, when souls are perishing from famine of the word, supply not the bread of grace which they have themselves received" (3.25). In the next sentence, he employs the pointed word "cursed" to refer to such neglectful pastors. Such daunting language is used "because through his fault of silence only he is condemned in the punishment of the many whom he might have corrected" (3.25).

Along with Purves, we can conclude that for Gregory "everyone who would be faithful in the work of pastoral care is faced with the concern for the state of his or her own soul and the quality of his or her own life before God."[14] Facing such a daunting and intimidating prospect for ministry, one would wonder, who is fit? Apparently though, even Gregory saw himself as unfit, for his work ends with this plea: "I have been as an ill-favored painter portraying a handsome man; and how I direct others to the shore of perfection, while myself still tossed among the waves of transgressions. But in the shipwreck of this present life sustain me, I beseech thee, by the

---

14. Purves, 67.

plank of thy prayer, that, since my own weight sinks me down, the hand of thy merit may raise me up" (4).

Gregory's highly influential document leaves one wondering: If he himself falls so short, who doesn't? Is there an unwritten grace behind his words, or are all pastors eternally hopeless?

PART TWO

Some English Pastoral Theologians

Chapter 4

A Thousand Years Later

Gregory of Nazianzus, John Chrysostom, and Gregory the Great shared in common the conviction that the pastoral ministry carries with it great demands and a host of spiritual hazards. Even the genre of the three documents tell a common story, as each one conveys a kind of defense of the author's original efforts to reject the call to pastoral ministry (the papacy in the case of Gregory the Great). Now we consider a body of English pastoral literature that appeared in the seventeenth and eighteenth centuries that share the same concern, but not the same story. During this period, the English church saw a notable number of its clergy re-sound the warnings that great spiritual risk accompanies the pastoral ministry; in fact, it is obvious that these English writers took their lead from the three earlier writers when addressing these spiritual hazards. Stated differently, the concerns of the English pastoral theologians regarding the hazards of ministry are traceable back to the first three documents examined. This is most clearly seen through the direct references some of the English writers make to the three earlier documents. For example, Gilbert Burnet, in his magisterial *Discourse of the Pastoral Care* (1692),[1] makes a direct reference to all three of the earlier writings, giving extensive attention to both Gregory of Nazianzus' Second Oration and John Chrysostom's *Six Books*.[2] Writing before Burnet, Richard Baxter shows the same awareness of this literature, twice directly quoting Gregory I, as well as employing one of

---

1. Gilbert Burnet, *A Discourse of the Pastoral Care* (1692), 56–76.

2. John Chrysostom, *De Sacerdotio* (AD 391), 6.13. Hereafter, all references will be cited in-text.

Gregory's vivid metaphors.³ In his visitation sermon, Bishop George Bull uses both Gregory of Nazianzus' and John Chrysostom's works to warn about the hazards that come with pastoral ministry.⁴

Yet another reason for tracing the source of the English pastoral theologians back to the earlier writers is that the repeated warnings of the former mirror the latter, indicating dependence. Even when not employing direct quotations, the warnings issued sound remarkably similar to those of the first three writers. Of particular significance is the repeated theme of accountability for the souls of the flock found in the earlier writings. This same theme is echoed by pastoral theologians like Burnet, who warns negligent pastors, "God will glorify himself by his severe judgments on them."⁵ Baxter seems confident his words actually apply to some pastors when he chides, "If you speak of hell, you speak of your own inheritance."⁶ Furthermore, these English writers demonstrate the same profound awareness of the deep hazards to the soul as did the earlier writers. George Herbert's concern over the "ghostly enemies" of spiritual pride and ambition are a direct reflection of our first three writers.⁷ Pastoral theologians not considered here also point to these issues, including Bishop Jeremy Taylor, who expresses concerns about vainglory, partiality, and conceit.⁸ This profound awareness of deep and "invisible" sin presents a great threat to the pastor, and arises first in the three writings already considered. It then re-emerges in the writings of the seventeenth and eighteenth century English pastoral theologians. When it comes to concerns regarding the spiritual hazards of pastoral ministry, the English writers demonstrate a consistent dependence on the first three of our writers. Regarding these issues, there is simply no other body of writing that appears to have had the same influence on them.

---

3. Richard Baxter, *The Reformed Pastor* (Edinburgh: The Banner of Truth Trust, 2005), 87.

4. George Bull, "A Visitation Sermon Concerning the Great Difficulties and Dangers of the Priestly Office" in *A Companion for the Candidates for Holy Orders* (1794), 14 & 32.

5. Burnet, 17.

6. Baxter, 54.

7. George Herbert, *The Country Parson, The Temple*, ed. John N. Wall, Jr., *The Classics of Western Spirituality* (New York: Paulist Press, 1981), 67.

8 Jeremy Taylor, *Rules and Advice to the Clergy of the Diocese of Down and Conner* (1663), 23.

Because of these realities, understanding the broad scope of the historical and theological background of Early Modern England is essential. Only against this backdrop will the rich texture and color of the pastoral advice appear in all its vividness. Since the writers we will consider span a specific period of time within the larger scope of the early modern era, our historical sketch will cover the late seventeenth century through the early eighteenth.

BACKGROUND

The period in which our authors lived and wrote was a time of tremendous change. When several of our authors were born, the world they knew was in the throes of the devastating Thirty Years War that ran between 1618 and 1648, an event that required decades for recovery. Meanwhile, the English watched with awe as the Americas were populated by their own, who in turn, threw a revolution that wrestled the colonies loose from their mother country. All the while, church and society were still readjusting to the tumult caused by the Protestant Reformation. To complicate matters, advances in science and medicine, along with new insights gained through philosophical inquiry, left Western Europe in the pains of tremendous change. Clearly, it was no longer the Middle Ages.

The English were profoundly affected by all of these changes. They had their own Reformation, albeit distinct in initial motive and manner from the changes that took place on the Continent. It was their colonies in America that eventually revolted, and after a brutal war, was granted its independence. For the people of the British Isles, it was also a time of sweeping change on the political landscape. It was the time of the reign of the Stuarts and the eventual Glorious Revolution that set the political and ecclesiastical climate for the next hundred years. It was also a period when the political and ecclesiastical spheres were greatly intertwined.

By the time our first writer entered the world, Elizabeth I had secured a State church with her Act of Uniformity (1559), which had effectively repealed Queen Mary's Catholic measures. The Act of Uniformity strategically fixed the Queen as head of the church, accompanied by Parliamentary acts forcing everyone, regardless of personal religious conviction, to conform. Some of the Protestants, however, were not satisfied. One such group, labeled "Puritans," were convinced that the Queen's changes fell drastically short of the reforms needed to align the church in

England with the will of God. While the Puritan movement would later experience a period of triumph, during the reign of Elizabeth, they were forced to abide with a church they believed to be only partly reformed. Elizabeth's reign, and the Tutor dynasty, came to an end upon her death in 1603, resulting in James VI of Scotland becoming James I of England. This was the beginning of the Stuart dynasty, led by a man the Puritans hoped would side with them; however, they were greatly disappointed, finding James lacking the slightest interest in promoting their agenda.

When the reign of James came to an end, his son, Charles, became Charles I, and took the throne in 1625. It was immediately apparent that this new King would be no friend to the Puritans or Independents. This resulted in an increasing divide between the king and nobles, on the one hand, and Parliament, the middle class, and the Puritans, on the other, since the Puritans had made successful inroads among the middle class. As the stealthy Puritans gained a gradual control over Parliament, Archbishop William Laud took increasingly brutal measures against these whom he saw as enemies of the church. Charles' call for Parliament to convene backfired on him. The now famous Long Parliament led to the 1640 impeachment of Charles' ally, Laud, the dismissal of the *Book of Common Prayer*, and the establishment of a Presbyterian form of government (that never saw full implementation). These decisions only led to increasing conflicts with the Monarch that culminated in a civil war and the overthrow of the king, who was eventually executed. Oliver Cromwell, head of the Parliamentary army rose to power, refused the kingship, and took the role of Lord Protector of the English Commonwealth.

Religiously, contrary to what some might assume of the Puritans, the Commonwealth provided significant religious leniency. Latourette comments, "Cromwell gave to England a nearer approach to religious liberty than it had thus far known."[9] Cromwell himself stood for a united state church, but one without bishops or the stipulations of the *Book of Common Prayer*. In fact, in Cromwell's view, save for the Quakers, all Protestants were to be tolerated.

At the death of Oliver Cromwell, anarchy threatened, and the Commonwealth was doomed. Together with most Presbyterians longing for social stability, the Royalists brought back the monarchy in the person of Charles' son, who would take the title, Charles II. Charles was not so ob-

---

9. Kenneth Scott Latourette, *A History of Christianity* (New York: Harper and Row, 1975), 2:823.

viously Catholic; in fact, he was "happy to ride two horses at the same time: Catholic in polity, Anglican in popular practice."[10] Although the new king was "thoroughly immoral, weak, and indifferent in religion,"[11] he rigidly demanded obedience, and quickly presented his own Act of Uniformity in 1662. His Act insisted on universal compliance and a firm adherence to the *Book of Common Prayer*; in effect, he restored the Church of England. His demands were clear: by St. Bartholomew's Day (August 24, 1662) all clergy had to swear an oath of allegiance to his Act. Two thousand refused to sign the oath, which led to what would soon be nicknamed the "Great Ejection." Adding insult to injury, Charles II then signed the Five Mile Act that forbade clergy who refused the oath from living within five miles of any incorporated city, including the city of his former place of ministry. It is this tightening of the screws that gave birth to English nonconformity; in a sense, the heirs of the Puritans. Nevertheless, some of England's most popular writers made their mark during the reign of Charles II: Richard Baxter, John Bunyan, and John Milton.

There was no question as to the religious persuasion of Charles' brother, King James, who came to power as James II in 1685. This second James would not be riding two horses at all; his horse was Roman Catholic only. In a veiled attempt to bring back Catholicism, James reversed Charles with a Declaration of Indulgence, giving toleration to both Catholics *and* Dissenters (1687). It was hoped that toleration of Dissenters would disguise his real intent of bringing back Catholicism. When James' wife bore a son, fears of a Catholic future began to haunt the minds of Anglicans, who put such pressure on the monarch that he was forced to flee England, paving the way for the Glorious Revolution.

It was James' own Protestant daughter, Mary, and her consort, William of Orange, along with an army, who set sail from the Netherlands to mount the throne of England. Their immediately established Bill of Rights reversed many of James' measures, stipulating that no Roman Catholic would ever be allowed on the throne of England. The Bill of Rights was followed by the Toleration Act of 1689, which permitted nonconformists to have their own public places of worship, and their own pastors, if they were willing to take an oath of loyalty and accept

---

10. William Gibson, *The Church of England, 1688–1822: Unity and Accord* (London: Routledge, 2001), 29.

11. Williston Walker, *A History of the Christian Church* (Edinburgh: T. & T. Clark, 1918), 474.

most of the Thirty-Nine Articles. Significantly, it was some four hundred *Anglican* clergy who refused to sign the oath based on their conviction that the ousted James retained the divine right to be king. Forming what was called the Non-Juror party, these English conservatives believed that good or no-good, James was the rightful occupant of the throne. In short, Gibson explains, although earlier James had acted from ulterior motives, "The Toleration Act essentially replaced James' broad religious indulgence with a narrower Protestant Trinitarian indulgence."[12]

On the heels of all this turmoil, there emerged two political parties. The Tories consisted of mostly squires and country parsons who opposed the toleration of dissenters (who made up about 10% of England's population at the time).[13] The Whigs were comprised mostly of town clergy, bishops, dissenters, and merchants. Yet in all of this change, the tremendous power of English religious and national sentiment can be seen by the fact that the Revolution was inspired by Anglican fears of James' Catholicity. "In this sense, the Church was the progenitor and midwife of the Revolution of 1688."[14] Thus, the eighteenth century that followed was an Anglican century, the stage being set by the Protestant Glorious Revolution. In fact, the long eighteenth century, as it is sometimes called because the period actually lasts from 1689–1832, "was marked by a strong sense of political, religious, cultural and national unity."[15]

Scrambling to find their footing during the sometimes violent ebb and flow of English politics and religion, the clergy, as a whole, nevertheless managed to perform their sacred duty. In fact, some were able rise above the tide to recognize the need for a solid core of future pastors. These were the men who expressed their advice in these books, letters, and sermons, which are the subjects of our present consideration. As we will see, these writers warned against vices such as spiritual pride, ambition, and impure hearts. They raised a warning flag over various temptations and discouragements, and reminded their fellow divines of their eternal accountability for the souls of their parishioners. But they also punctuated their warnings with an insistence on forming certain habits to shield pastors from the hazards of professional ministry. It would

12. Gibson, 62.
13. Walker, 477.
14. Gibson, 61.
15. Ibid., 242.

certainly be the opinion of these pastoral writers that this ministry is "an alien work that demands great transformation by God, for the want of which the work of the pastor cannot succeed. In fact, the lack of interior renewal will lead to an outward ministry that will likely destroy both the pastor and his or her congregation."[16]

THE ENGLISH PASTORAL THEOLOGICAL LITERATURE

The body of literature that constitutes books, letters, and sermons of advice to pastors is vast enough to construct a taxonomy. Building on an unpublished taxonomy by James Bradley, we can see that there are at least five categories.[17] First, formal full-length treatises. The two early works that are most notable examples are George Herbert's *A Priest to the Temple*, or *The Country Parson* (1632), and Richard Baxter's *The Reformed Pastor* (1655). Five formal, full-length treatises under our present concern are Gilbert Burnet's *A Discourse of the Pastoral Care* (1692), John Mason's *Student and Pastor* (1755), Isaac Watts' *An Humble Attempt Towards the Revival of Practical Religion* (1731), Henry Norris' *A Manual for the Parish Priest* (1815), and Henry Owen's *Directions for Young Students in Divinity* (1810).

The second category suggested by Bradley is comprised of visitation charges delivered by bishops to the clergy of their various dioceses. There are a number of these extant, such as Jeremy Taylor's *Rules and Advice to the Clergy* (1661) and Thomas Secker's *Eight Charges to the Clergy* (1769). Included here is Bishop George Bull's 1708 visitation sermon found in his *Companion for Candidates for Holy Orders* (1714).

Third are letters of advice penned by more mature pastors in an effort to give direction to younger pastors. These letters might include personal letters, such as Adam Clarke's *A Letter to a Preacher* (1812), or general letters intended for the larger audience, such as John Clubbe's *A Letter of Free Advice to a Young Clergyman* (1765).

Following this are the anthologies that begin to appear in the early nineteenth century, sometimes identified with an author, sometimes containing the works of several authors. *The Clergyman's Instructor*, for

---

16. Andrew Purves, *Pastoral Theology in the Classical Tradition* (Louisville: Westminster John Knox, 2001), 118.

17. James Bradley, "The Institutions and Literature of Formation," (Lecture, Fuller Theological Seminary, Malibu, CA, October 15, 2007).

instance, contains eight major treatises collected together, while *The Young Minister's Companion* is composed of the advice of nonconforming ministers. Finally, there are a few manuals for wives of clergymen, one even written by a woman. Louisa Clark's *The Country Parson's Wife* was meant to go along with George Herbert's immensely popular book of similar title.

There is one further category that might be added to the list since two of our present works defy the above-named categories. A sixth category could be called "Occasional Sermons." These are not sermons preached by a bishop to his clergy, but other sermons preached by non-bishop clergy on various occasions. Neither of William Paley's works under consideration here fit into any of the aforementioned categories, for they are simply occasional sermons: *Advice Addressed to the Young Clergy of the Dioceses of Carlisle* (1781), and *Dangers Incidental to the Clerical Character* (1766).

The heart of this work focuses on the contributions six writers make to the theme of pastoral hazards and the challenges ministers face in overcoming them. Others writings could have been examined, but these authors represent a broad swath of English pastors serving from the mid-seventeenth to the end of the eighteenth centuries. Furthermore, they each present a unique angle on the present concern. Just as it was important to develop an historical background to this material, it is equally important to understand the stories of the authors and preachers themselves, for when these two pieces are woven together, one better appreciates the significance of the contributions they made and appreciate the timelessness of their wisdom.

Thus, the second part of this book falls into two major sections. The first focuses on three book-length treatises presented in chronological order, beginning with a brief look at one section of George Herbert's famous *Country Parson*. Following Herbert is a more extensive look at two books from the seventeenth century. The treatment of these is more extensive because of the sheer amount of material in them that is significant to our concern. The first work is Richard Baxter's 1656 classic, *The Reformed Pastor*, which expresses tremendous concern over the issue of pastoral spiritual health. Next, we discover the same concerns scattered throughout the contribution Bishop Gilbert Burnet makes in his 1692, *A Discourse of the Pastoral Care*.

The second section builds on three English pastoral sermons significant to our concern. Again, taken chronologically, we begin with George Bull's "Visitation Sermon," delivered in 1708, which is entirely concerned with the present issue. We round out our survey of pertinent English sermons by observing the very unique contribution made by William Paley in his "Dangers Incidental to the Clerical Character" (1795).

Chapter 5

George Herbert

But is first a sermon to himself, and then to others.

The acclaimed seventeenth-century Anglican priest and poet, still studied by literary scholars for his brilliant word craft, was first of all a pastor. While Herbert's clear object in *The Country Parson* was "to set down the form and character of a true pastor,"[1] his intention in his beautiful poetic works was not altogether different. "In his poems, as in his priestly duties, Herbert understands his role as that of 'the Deputy of Christ for the reducing of Man to the Obedience of God.'"[2] It is common knowledge that his influence over the past three centuries has been great. Even Richard Baxter, that paragon of Puritan virtue, and near contemporary of Herbert, was affected by Herbert's poetical works: "Herbert speaks to God like one that really believeth in God, and whose business in the world is most with God. *Heart-work* and *Heaven-work* make up his book."[3]

However, Herbert was no Puritan. He defended blessings, which Puritans dismissed as "Popish;" he retained priestly confession and the use of the cross, and heavily relied upon the *Book of Common Prayer*. In fact, the *Book* "was at the heart of Herbert's life and teaching."[4] Sheldrake

---

1. George Herbert, *The Country Parson, The Temple*, ed. John N. Wall, Jr., *The Classics of Western Spirituality* (New York: Paulist Press, 1981), 54.

2. John N. Wall, Jr., introduction to *The Country Parson, The Temple,* ed. John N. Wall, Jr., *The Classics of Western Spirituality* (New York: Paulist Press, 1981), 35.

3. Cited in preface to Herbert, xiii.

4. Philip Sheldrake, "George Herbert and *The Country Parson*" in *A History of Pastoral*

concludes that Herbert "was typical of most non-Puritan divines of his time in accepting aspects of Calvinist doctrine while not being straightforward a Calvinist."[5] To Herbert, the prayers of his congregation, both public and private, were central to church life. Faithfully appearing each day to lead his people in the canonical hours at 10:00 and 4:00, he had a profound effect on his parishioners, even though, by doing so, he was clearly demarcating himself as a non-Puritan. J. William Black is a bit more precise in pinpointing Herbert's convictions on the contemporary theological continuum: "Herbert was much more an Elizabethan Settlement Protestant than he was of either the puritan or Laudian parties."[6]

George Herbert was marked out as one of Westminster School's "illustrious students" in his earliest education.[7] From Westminster, he matriculated into Trinity College, Cambridge, and there distinguished himself again, first taking the BA in 1613 and then the MA three years later. Being elected Major Fellow of Trinity, Herbert also entered into studies in pursuit of the Bachelor of Divinity, only to delay ordination to serve in Parliament. Married to Jane Danvers on March 5, 1629, a woman of noble family roots, it was not until April 26, 1630 that Herbert was installed as rector of St. Andrew's Church in Bemerton. His ordination took place at Salisbury Cathedral later that year. Sadly, Herbert's ministry there would last only three years, for on March 1, 1633, Herbert died of consumption.

THE COUNTRY PARSON

"I have resolved to set down the form and character of a true pastor, that I may have a mark to aim at."[8] In his rather straightforward portrayal of his purpose, Herbert makes it obvious that his desire is to write out an ideal picture of what the pastor is to do and who the pastor is to be. Although intended for every pastor, Herbert admits that his work sets out a target from which he himself falls somewhat short. From this humble confession, Herbert launches into what would become "the most comprehensive published analysis of the pastor's duty that Protestant England

---

Care, ed. GR Evans (London: Cassell, 2000), 299.

5. Ibid., 296.

6. J William Black, *Reformation Pastors: Richard Baxter and the Ideal of the Reformed Pastor* (Carlisle: Paternoster Press, 2004), 48.

7. Wall, 13.

8. Herbert, 54.

had seen,"⁹ first published in 1652. Sheldrake considers it a work of rhetoric that is motivated by two factors.¹⁰ First, he wants to *move* his readers rather than to simply *instruct* his readers. His hope is that the reader will experience a deepened sense of call as opposed to simply gaining more head-knowledge. Second, Herbert wants his pastor-readers to themselves be motivated to a rhetorical approach to ministry; he wants other pastors to *move* their parishioners to a greater faith. Herbert's intentions were obviously met with great success. In fact, those who dismissed Gilbert Burnet's *Discourse of the Pastoral Care* (1692) because of the author's involvement in thorny ecclesiastical issues, turned to Herbert, who chose not to involve himself in such controversies.¹¹ But for Herbert, his work as a country parson was a job unlike any other; it was an all-consuming way of life with his own personal holiness at the center.

Taking a lead from Philip Sheldrake, there are at least six lasting contributions from Herbert's *The Country Parson*.¹² First, the work of ministry is a way of life; it is not only an activity. Second, pastoral care requires balancing both detachment and engagement. Third, the ministry is profoundly spiritual in the deepest sense imaginable—it is not a form of social work. Fourth, the work of pastoral ministry is not just communicated through raw knowledge; his use of poetry shows that insight and growth come from realities far deeper than the rational or conceptual. Fifth, pastoral care is not only an individual work, but a work carried out for those in community. Sixth, pastoral ministry is holistic because it touches all areas of human life, not simply the religious. These insights we owe, in part, to the work of George Herbert.

In his signal ninth chapter, titled "The Parson's State of Life," Herbert rehearses the lofty calling that comes with pastoral ministry. The priest is preferably unmarried, his deportment very serious and self-conscious, and he is religiously observant beyond the highest standard.¹³ Indeed, his body is healthful and his soul, fervent. The standard is high: "To put on

---

9. Black, 48.

10. Sheldrake, 297.

11. Donald A. Spaeth, *The Church in the Age of Danger: Parsons and Parishoners 1660–1740* in Cambridge Studies in Early Modern British History, eds. Anthony Fletcher, John Guy, and John Morrill (Cambridge: Cambridge University Press, 2000), 109.

12. Sheldrake, 310.

13. Herbert, 66.

the profound humility, and the exact temperance of our Lord Jesus."[14] It may help the intimidated reader at this point to be reminded that *The Country Parson* represents a "mark to aim at."

It is in this context that Herbert begins to surface various hazards that the pastor/priest must also face in carrying out his sacred duty. He mentions two "peculiar" temptations, which he labels "ghostly enemies."[15] First is the oft-mentioned bane of pastoral ministry, spiritual pride; the other, an impure heart. Without defining these sins of ministry, like a true rhetorician, he implores the priest to gird his loins, keep his imagination in check, and put on the full armor of God. In so doing, the pastor needn't be afraid of these twin evils. However, Herbert is not finished, for he immediately highlights "other temptations" which are like "mortal enemies."[16] Ambition, for one, creates mischief, especially among those who are single. This "untimely desire of promotion to an higher state" is marked by a willingness to accommodate oneself or repay one's benefactor.[17] Curiosity is another temptation peculiar to priests, especially those unmarried. Without further comment, Herbert explains that curiosity is "prying into high speculative and unprofitable questions, alluring to those in this scholarly profession."[18] The married pastor is by no means immune from temptation, only the nature of those temptations change in his case. His temptations may be understood to be more domestic; the kind that lures him into covetousness, love of pleasure, or ease.

It would be inaccurate to conclude that this is the only chapter in which Herbert addresses the spiritual concerns inherent in ministry. Elsewhere, he takes up a common warning in the English pastoral literature to make sure that the pastor looks first to himself (or "herself"), "For in preaching to others, he forgets not himself, but is first a sermon to himself, and then to others; growing with the growth of his parish."[19] Obviously then, the high call of the pastor to exhibit "the exact temperance of our Lord Jesus," really is a mark to aim at, for the pastor is himself (or herself) in the growth process, as is the case with the whole parish.

14. Ibid.
15. Ibid.
16. Ibid.
17. Ibid.
18. Ibid.
19. Ibid., 83

This great aim is of no little importance or difficulty; indeed, "the greatest and hardest preparation is within."[20]

Herbert's profoundly influential book begs the question of what would have flowed from his pen had he been allowed more earthly years. All speculation aside, what we have been given from the pen of this great seventeenth-century parson is rich enough to provide most pastors with a series of life-time challenges.

20. Ibid., 56.

CHAPTER 6

Richard Baxter

For your people's sakes, therefore, look to your hearts.

To survey the story of Richard Baxter is to scan the story of English Puritanism, for Baxter's life reflects the ebb and flow of that sixteenth- and seventeenth-century English movement. Therefore, in order to more fully grasp the riches of his renowned book, *The Reformed Pastor*, one should have a more specific understanding of the story and ethos of English Puritanism, although it must be acknowledged that the nature and even coherence of Puritanism has been the subject of considerable scholarly debate.[1]

Even though "Calvinism was accepted orthodoxy in Elizabeth's reign," her 1559 Act of Uniformity failed by falling short of the Calvinist ideal.[2] To be sure, Elizabeth's act had repealed all the legislation of Catholic Queen Mary, but certain ecclesiastical dress and ornaments were still required, and Elizabeth retained the right to introduce ceremonies and other rites. Issues like these did not sit well with some Protestants who had expected greater changes. These were the "Puritans," so-called in part because of their insistence on a complete break with Rome and all things associated with it.

---

1. See Francis J. Bremer, ed., *Puritanism: Transatlantic Perspectives on a Seventeenth-Century Anglo-American Faith* (Boston: Massachusetts Historical Society, 1993).

2. Doreen Rosman, *The Evolution of the English Churches: 1500–2000* (Cambridge University Press, 2003), 60.

In an attempt to press their case, certain like-minded Puritans gathered together to formulate an admonition rejecting "popish" remnants, which they delivered to the Queen in 1572. A follow-up admonition outraged the Queen. Elizabeth, though herself a Protestant, would not tolerate dissent, and demanded complete compliance, fearing political upheaval without it. The Puritans were met with the Conventicle Act of 1593, which imposed imprisonment or banishment on those who failed to comply. That Act directly resulted in many Puritans fleeing first to Holland, with some ultimately sailing to the New World.

Elizabeth's successor, James I, demonstrated a willingness to agree to minor Puritan reforms, but this was only part of the larger political and religious struggle he faced, for "much of seventeenth-century politics can be told in terms of competing impulses to advance, complete, or reverse the Reformation."[3] In fact, as Andrew Purves notes, all of the major religious factions looked to James with hope.[4] The Catholics held out hope because of his mother, Mary, Queen of Scots, the Presbyterian Puritans because of his Scottish upbringing, and the Anglicans because of his known antipathy toward Presbyterianism. Adding encouragement to Puritan hope, it was this Monarch who sent a delegation to the Synod of Dort, a delegation that sided with Puritan Calvinist convictions.

Despite the fact that Puritanism finally won the day after the defeat of Charles I, its lifespan as a dominant movement turned out to be short-lived. England, it seems, was destined to be a monarchy, for in 1660, Parliament invited Charles II to the throne, and England celebrated its great Restoration. Not surprisingly, the Restoration caused some Puritans to flee to New England, and the rest to attempt to adjust to the newly enforced changes. Charles II's 1662 Act of Uniformity outlawed all religious expression other than Anglican, which naturally created a group of vocal dissenters. When, on St. Bartholomew's Day, all dissenters were officially ousted from the Church of England, clergy were left to find work either as schoolmasters, chaplains, or physicians. Others who persisted in preaching, like John Bunyan, paid the price with a series of imprisonments.

Charles II was replaced by his younger, and staunchly Catholic, brother James II who eventually had to flee for his life because of

---

3. John Spurr, *The Post-Reformation: Religion, Politics, and Society in Britain, 1603–1714* (New York: Pearson Longman, 2006), 35.

4. Andrew Purves, *Pastoral Theology in the Classical Tradition* (Louisville: Westminster John Knox, 2001), 97.

Anglican resistance. When William and Mary came to the throne, their Act of Toleration allowed dissenter groups such and Baptists, Congregationalists, and Presbyterians to worship as they chose. These very strands had emerged from the earlier dissenting groups collectively condemned as "Puritans;" "Those who stood for Calvinism-emphasizing the duties of the elect and practicing a sparse religious service centered on the preaching of the Word . . . ."[5]

Puritanism then, J. I. Packer defines "as that movement in sixteenth- and seventeenth-century England which sought further reformation and renewal in the Church of England than the Elizabethan settlement allowed."[6] It was a movement marked by three identifying characteristics. First, it was marked by certain Calvinist theological convictions, which amounted to a particular self-understanding. In the words of Rosman, as Calvinists, the Puritans were convinced that "they were not saved because they believed, but believed because they were saved."[7] Second, these Calvinist-convicted Puritans all shared the desire to rid the Church of England of "popery." They adamantly believed that every last element of Catholic worship and government must be eliminated. The removal of these elements, it was thought, would bring the church closer to its purer, New Testament roots. Third, the Puritans held "a shared literature, catechetical, evangelistic and devotional, with a homiletical style and experiential emphasis that were all its own."[8]

Of all Puritan writers, Packer believes that Richard Baxter was its "most distinguished."[9] Born in 1615 to a family Baxter confesses was "addicted to gaming,"[10] young Richard showed a promising intellectual propensity, but was educated simply in country schools. Returning home after a brief period of study at Ludlow (in lieu of a university education), Baxter took over as schoolmaster back at his early school in Wroxeter.

---

5. Francis Bremer, *Shaping New Englands: Puritan Clergymen in Seventeenth-Century England and New England*, Twayne's United States Author Series, ed. Pattie Cowell (New York: Twayne Publishers, 1994), 7.

6. J. I. Packer, *A Quest for Godliness* (Wheaton: Crossway Books, 1990), 35.

7. Rosman, 61.

8. Packer, 36.

9. Ibid.

10. Richard Baxter, *The Autobiography of Richard Baxter*, Everyman's Library, ed. Ernest Rhys (London: JM Dent & Sons, 1931), 3.

Indeed, Baxter was always a kind of schoolmaster, although he openly admitted his academic deficiencies.[11]

In his early adulthood, beset by severe questions over his salvation, Baxter was plunged into existential despair. His peace came through the ministry itself, for, as he discovered, in answering others' spiritual anxieties, he answered his own. At age 21, Baxter was assaulted by an illness for over a year. So intense was his anguish that he feared for his life and found himself under divine compulsion to accomplish "men's" conversion. In other words, his sickness drove his ministry. Eventually ordained, he began his formal ministry teaching school, during which time he preached his first sermon, and became a fledgling non-conformist.

Baxter's life would change, and so would many other lives for years to come, by his call to the parish at Kidderminster in 1641. His appointment to Kidderminster was prompted by congregational complaints against their present vicar, a man who "understood not the very substantial Articles of Christianity . . . frequented alehouses and had sometimes been drunk."[12] Initially, his ministry there lasted only a year due to an interval of nearly six years in the Civil War. Purves explains that Kidderminster was a Royalist town, and because of Baxter's support for Parliament and the Puritan cause, he was compelled to leave.[13] Upon invitation to serve as a chaplain to the parliamentary forces, Baxter entered Army life, a life for which he was not particularly well-suited due to ill health. Such problems led to his departure from the army and his return to the parish at Kidderminster in 1647.

Kidderminster was a village with some four thousand inhabitants, including the surrounding area, amounting to some eight hundred families. Baxter's ambitious visitation plan was no small feat. Besides preaching on the Lord's-day, preaching once on Thursday, holding sermon discussions at his home on Thursday evenings, and praying with a group each Saturday evening, Baxter states: "Every week my assistant and I myself took fourteen families between us for private catechizing and conference . . . ."[14] It was this systematic congregational care that gave rise to *The Reformed Pastor*.

---

11. Ibid., 9.
12. Ibid., 24.
13. Purves, 100.
14. Baxter, 78.

Despite his great efforts, the Kidderminster ministry did not end peacefully. Forced out by a growing number of "sectaries" in 1660, Baxter found himself without a living, although he was later able to express with satisfaction that his ministry had left many "grown up to some confirmedness and maturity . . . ."[15] Sadly, for the remaining thirty years of his life, Baxter never held a regular pastorate. He was married in 1662 to one Margaret Charlton, who helped support his private preaching and eventual writing, since the Act of Uniformity that year led to his exclusion from the Church of England. Despite two imprisonments and continued struggles with his health, Baxter lived a full life of seventy-six years.

Baxter left behind a series of writings impressive in number. Andrew Purves reports 135 written during his lifetime.[16] Of special note is *The Saint's Everlasting Rest*, first published in 1650. His "vast, encyclopedic"[17] *Christian Directory* was published in 1673. It is his *Reformed Pastor*, though, that was most often read, and remains in print some 350 years after first being published in 1656.

In spite of its great popularity, Richard Baxter is not without his detractors. C. Fitzsimons Allison, for one, takes Baxter's theology of justification to task, pointing out that Baxter's 1649 *Aphorisms of Justification* embroiled him in a life-long controversy over that doctrine.[18] In short, Allison contends that Baxter's doctrine amounts to the believer being required to fulfill their end of covenant responsibilities *in order to* receive legal righteousness; thus, the believer is justified by his or her own performed righteousness.[19] Allison concludes: "Baxter is, then, in accord with the 'holy living' Anglicans that faith includes obedience and charity, that the new covenant is more lenient than the old, that Christ's righteousness is the meritorious and not the formal cause of justification, and that antinomianism is to be shunned by an emphasis upon holy living."[20]

Despite the controversy over justification that followed Baxter throughout his life, it is almost difficult to overstate the impact of The

15. Ibid., 84.

16. Purves, 100.

17. David Cornick, "Pastoral Care in England," in *A History of Pastoral Care*, ed. GR Evans (London: Cassell, 2000), 315.

18. C. Fitzsimons Allison, *The Rise of Moralism* (Vancouver: Regent College Publishing, 2003), 154.

19 Ibid., 157.

20. Ibid. 158.

Reformed Pastor. In his introduction to Banner of Truth's edition to *The Reformed Pastor*, J. I. Packer lauds Baxter's pastoral expertise. Baxter is "the most outstanding pastor, evangelist and writer on practical and devotional themes that Puritanism produced."[21] This complement is more pronounced when one considers Packer's aversion to some of Baxter's theological particularities, many of which are spelled out in Allison's work.[22] Obviously, Packer is not the only one to have praised Baxter's work, for in his introduction, he cites various other accolades by repeating the long list found in J. T. Wilkinson's 1939 edition of the same book.[23]

THE REFORMED PASTOR

The work that became known as The Reformed Pastor grew out of an invitation Baxter received to preach to fellow clergy about the great ministry of pastoral catechism. Baxter describes the situation both in his autobiography and the book itself. From his autobiography: "When we set upon this great work [catechizing] it was thought best to begin with a day of fasting and prayer by all the ministers at Worcester, where they desired me to preach. But weakness and other things hindered me from that day; but to compensate that I enlarged and published the sermon which I had prepared for them, and entitled the treatise Gildas Silvanus (because I imitated Gildas and Salvianus in my liberty of speech to the pastors of the churches), or The Reformed Pastor . . . .[24]" He then proceeds to identify the heart of his concern in this lecture, turned book: "If God would but reform the ministry, and set them on their duties zealously and faithfully, the people would certainly be reformed. All churches either rise or fall as the ministry doth rise or fall."[25] In different words, from *The Reformed Pastor* itself: "What speedier way is there for the depraving and undoing of the people, than the depravity of their guides?"[26] So Baxter's book is

---

21. J. I. Packer, introduction to *The Reformed Pastor,* by Richard Baxter (Edinburgh: The Banner of Truth Trust, 2005), 9.

22. Packer, *Quest,* 157ff.

23. Packer, introduction to *The Reformed Pastor,* 14.

24. Baxter, *Autobiography,* 97.

25. Ibid., 97.

26. Richard Baxter, *The Reformed Pastor* (Edinburgh: The Banner of Truth Trust, 2005), 39. There are various versions of Baxter's work in print, most of which are abridged to one degree or another. Thus, it should be noted that my references to chapters and sections are directly tied to the Banner of Truth edition.

based upon Acts 20.28: "Take heed therefore unto yourselves, and to all the flock, over which the Holy Ghost hath made you overseers, to feed the church of God, which he hath purchased with his own blood." As Purves puts it: "Transformed ministry comes from transformed pastors."[27] Again, Purves notes that Baxter "is more concerned with the pastor's life in God than with the parishioner's, because adequate attention to the latter is possible only by one who has paid attention to the former."[28]

As to the title itself, as most commentators are careful to point out, "Reformed" does not refer to a specific theological bent. Packer notes that in the original edition of the work, "Reformed" appears larger than any other word, giving it central significance, but the word really means "revived."[29] Purves defines the reformed pastor as the "spiritually renewed" pastor.[30]

Baxter's own simplified outline will suffice to orient us to his work.[31] First, it is his intention to consider what it is to take heed to oneself. Second, he wants to show *why* one must take heed. He then begins to shift attention to the flock, for third, he begins to inquire what it means to take heed to the flock. Fourth, he wants to illustrate the manner in which one must take heed, followed by, fifth, the motives for taking heed. Finally, it is Baxter's stated desire to make some application of all of this.

True to Puritan practice, Baxter's work is full of itemized lists, and one list seems to overlap another. It is also replete with warnings, not unlike Gregory the Great's *Book of Pastoral Rule*, a work he directly quotes. In a very pointed passage, Baxter exhorts: "We have the same sins to mortify, and the same graces to be quickened and strengthened, as our people have: we have greater works to do than they have, and greater difficulties to overcome, and therefore we have need to be warned and awakened, if not to be instructed, as well as they . . . ."[32] Our purpose leads us to focus primarily on the section he entitled, "The Motives for this Oversight" (of ourselves), while making some reference back to section one, "The Nature of this Oversight."

To begin with, Baxter warns that pastors must take heed to themselves, lest in preaching to others, the pastor neglect his (or her) own

---

27. Purves, 104.
28. Ibid., 105.
29. Packer, *Quest*, 13.
30. Purves, 105.
31. Baxter, *The Reformed Pastor*, 52.
32. Ibid., 51.

self.[33] Simply put, "It concerneth you to begin at home."[34] Employing a rather daunting reference to the end of Matthew 25, Baxter wants to warn his fellow pastors that in the end, some will call on the Lord, but the Lord will not recognize them. "And all because we preached so many sermons of Christ, while we neglected him; of the Spirit, while we resisted him; of faith, while we did not ourselves believe; of repentance and conversion, while we continued in an impenitent and unconverted state; and of a heavenly life, while we remained carnal and earthly ourselves."[35] Indeed, "a holy calling will not save an unholy man."[36] To be sure, this is an echo of an earlier warning. In the first section, where he describes what it is to take heed to oneself, he wrote, "take heed to yourselves, lest you be void of that saving grace of God which you offer to others."[37] There he states that this pastor must be one who does not live in open sin but lives a life of good works. His concern is clearly the danger of churches being served by pastors who personally have not tasted of the grace of God: "Alas! It is the common danger and calamity of the Church, to have unregenerate and inexperienced pastors, and to have so many men become preachers before they are Christians; who are sanctified by dedication to the altar as the priests of God, before they are sanctified by hearty dedication as the disciples of Christ; and so to worship an unknown God, and to preach an unknown Christ, to pray through an unknown Spirit, to recommend a state of holiness and communion with God, and a glory and happiness which are all unknown, and like to be unknown to them forever."[38]

Baxter's fear is clearly based on the danger of placing those in ministry leadership who have no real personal experience with the grace of God in Jesus Christ. Perhaps he imagines a young, articulate, gifted and friendly student, who is thrust up front by leaders charging that person with a call to ministry before that one truly claims Christ. Baxter probably could not have envisioned the "converted" celebrity who finds himself or herself on the preaching circuit before the seed has truly planted,

---

33. Again, in employing the masculine pronoun, I am reflecting the language of Baxter and others in his day regarding strict role differentiation for males and females. To honor the current status of women in ministry, I use the feminine in parentheses.

34. Baxter, *The Reformed Pastor*, 72.

35. Ibid.

36. Ibid., 73.

37. Ibid., 53.

38. Ibid., 56.

but this might be a contemporary expression of his concern. It is with wisdom and foresight then, that Baxter warns, "Preach to yourselves the sermons which you study."[39] The pastor must attend to himself (or herself), Baxter proclaims, or others will suffer for it: "Lest you be guilty of what daily you condemn."[40]

It is in the context of Baxter's passionate desire for pastors to exercise self care that he twice quotes Gregory I. In his section on the nature of pastoral oversight, he leans on Gregory's timeless wisdom with the first of two direct quotations: "He cannot succeed in healing the wounds of others who is himself unhealed by reason of neglecting himself. He neither benefits his neighbors nor himself. He does not raise up others, but himself falls."[41] Underscoring this awareness and clear dependence upon Gregory, he goes on to provide an even more extensive quotation from an earlier section of the *Rule*.[42] Here he warns of the pastor who undermines true ministry by either teaching without careful meditation or conducting life in a way inconsistent with the gospel. It is these who must be careful not to move forward in a "headstrong manner" and defeat their own work, which happens when they "proclaim in public what they impugn by their conduct." Even Baxter's next line is a paraphrase of Gregory: "When we have led them to living water, if we muddy it by our filthy lives, we may lose our labour, and they be never the better."[43]

Baxter warns his readers, secondly, to keep watch, for the pastor has a depraved nature just like everyone else. His point of reference here is Adam, who was innocent, but still fell into depravity. How much greater need have we, who come into ministry with a nature already depraved? Baxter does not mince words in addressing the evil heart: "Alas! in our hearts, as well as in our hearers, there is an averseness to God, a strangeness to him, unreasonable and almost unruly passions!"[44] Similarly, in the first chapter he notes that when one "little" sin is allowed entry, others march right on in, for "great distempers and apostasies have usually small beginnings."[45]

---

39. Ibid., 61.
40. Ibid., 67.
41. Ibid., 87. The Gregory quotation is taken from book 4 of the *Book of Pastoral Rule*.
42. Ibid. This quotation is found in *N&PNF*, 1.2.
43. Ibid. The wording here directly reflects Gregory's use of the same imagery in 1.2.
44. Ibid., 73.
45. Ibid., 62.

All of this is rooted in this innate strangeness to God. Here he warns of the corollary "pang of spiritual pride" that can so easily overtake and cause one to want to draw away disciples to himself.[46] This being the case, the call is to take a long and frequent look into one's own heart. Since pastoral sins always take others with it, Baxter urges his readers: "For your people's sakes, therefore, look to your hearts."[47]

We observe a third warning from Baxter that sounds very similar to Chrysostom. The pastor must beware, because the tempter will attack him (or her) with greater effort and tenacity than he will attack another. For Baxter, the issue here is that the pastor is the one who leads the charge against Satan, so naturally, the pastor will be the greatest target. "He [Satan] beareth the greatest malice to those that are engaged to do him the greatest mischief."[48] In fact, it is the intention of the Prince of Darkness to attack the pastor because "he knows what a rout he may make among them, if the leaders fall before their eyes."[49] With words just as intimidating as any of Baxter's others, he warns pastors to "take heed, therefore, brethren, for the enemy hath a special eye on you."[50]

How does the enemy accomplish this grand scheme? According to Baxter, Satan has incredible skill that makes him difficult to outwit. He warns the pastor that Satan is a better scholar and possesses greater rhetorical skills. Think of the success the devil will have, imagines Baxter, if he can "make" the minister lazy or unfaithful. What a conquest if the pastor falls into covetousness or scandal. Like a platoon leader activating his troops, Baxter implores his fellow ministers to fight the fight and not give up ground.

Fourth, "take heed to yourselves, because there are many eyes upon you and there will be many to observe your faults."[51] Very simply, as Baxter reflects in other places, the pastor does not sin in isolation. Like the sun in full eclipse cannot help but still be noticed, the pastor must beware that he (or she) is in the same position. This reality, however, Baxter considers a blessing, for this puts a certain restraint on our evil nature that others

46. Ibid.
47. Ibid.
48. Ibid., 74.
49. Ibid.
50. Ibid.
51. Ibid., 75.

do not have. Interestingly, behind this warning is Baxter's clear conviction that the world is not only watching, but it watches with ulterior motives. The world watches with "a malicious mind"; they are "ready to make the worst of it all."[52] Indeed, they want to "find the smallest" fault where it is, to aggravate it where they find it, to divulge it and to take advantage of it to their own designs, and to make faults where they cannot find them. How cautiously, then, should we walk before so many ill-minded observers!"[53]

Given Baxter's conviction that all pastors are being watched and are fixed in Satan's sites, he expresses a fifth warning: The pastor must take heed, for his (or her) sins have greater consequence. In this context, he is not calling attention to the public impact of their sins, which he has already addressed, but simply because the person has a great calling, their sins have great consequences. So he begins by quoting a saying he attributes to King Alphonsus: "A great man cannot commit a small sin."[54] Here he makes three sub-points. First, the pastor is more likely to commit sins against knowledge. Because you know more, he warns his hearers, you will be responsible for more. The reverse should be the case; since the pastor knows more, his will to obey should be greater. Second, the sinning pastor is a greater hypocrite than someone else. "O what a heinous thing is it in us, to study how to disgrace sin to the utmost, and make it as odious in the eyes of our people as we can, and when we have done, to live in it, and secretly cherish that which we publicly disgrace!"[55] Hypocrisy is greater when the one who preaches against the evils of sin, himself engages in it. Baxter asks, "Did you think as ill of sin as you spoke, or did you not?"[56] Third, to further his point that a pastor's sins have greater consequence, Baxter understands that all pastoral acts are a repudiation of sin; thus, one sin undermines all pastoral acts. So, the pastor's sins have more "perfidiousness" in them; there is greater betrayal and violation of faith when he trespasses than when others do. This is nothing less than "treachery."[57]

In this second chapter, Baxter goes on to make three last points. Sixth on his list of issues that should cause a careful pastor to take heed, is that

52. Ibid., 76.
53. Ibid.
54. Ibid.
55. Ibid., 76, 77.
56. Ibid., 77.
57. Ibid.

the pastor's work requires greater grace. The tone of this point is noticeably different than the others, in that it is less a rebuke and more a gentle exhortation. Nevertheless, it is a warning rooted in the reality that pastors go through greater trials than do others, so greater grace is needed. The pastor must always be vigilant: "Do not think that a heedless, careless course will accomplish so great a work as this."[58] This very problem can be seen in other employments wherein a military official, for instance, is placed in a role too great for his gifts or character. "If, then, you will venture into the midst of enemies, and bear the burden of the heat of the day, take heed to yourselves."[59]

Baxter articulates his seventh point: "As you may render him more service, so you may do him more disservice than others."[60] In Baxter's mind, the pastor stands nearer to God than others, so the pastor can bring greater honor to God, or cause greater dishonor. To Baxter, the honor of God has been entrusted to the pastor to uphold with his (or her) very life. The pastor's life, then, can bring defame on God: "Could your hearts endure to hear me cast the dung of your iniquities in the face of holy God?"[61] The case Baxter makes begins with a biblical reference to the sons of Eli who endured the wrath of God for their careless rebellion against him. Behind this example, though, is the fact that their priestly role puts them nearer to God than is the case with others. It is the same issue that caused God to deal so severely with David. To live in open sin and reap the mockery of outsiders would be dung thrown into the face of God. Key to understanding the uniqueness of Baxter's seventh point is his exhortation, "You are entrusted with his honour!"[62] By virtue of the minister's position, because of what he (or she) represents, all disgrace is a direct mockery of God himself. "O take heed, brethren, of every word you speak, and of every step you tread, for you bear the ark of the Lord . . . ."[63]

Aside from his first point, Baxter's final point is his longest. Here, our author urges pastors to watch out, for if the work God does is not having an impact on the heart of the pastor himself (or herself), that pastor can-

---

58. Ibid., 78.
59. Ibid.
60. Ibid.
61. Ibid., 79.
62. Ibid.
63. Ibid.

not expect an impact on anyone else's heart. To be sure, Baxter clarifies, God continues to do his work in and through the heart of an unfaithful pastor, but there is reason for concern: "God doth more seldom prosper the labours of unsanctified men."[64] Typical for a Puritan, Baxter then elucidates with four sub-points. First, he argues that unregenerate persons do not make God their chief aim, nor do they do anything heartily for his glory. Only the converted pastor works from such motivation. He explains that many end up in pastoral work for reasons other than a genuine call. These, Baxter clarifies, are only in it for themselves, so they operate out of their own strength, making it impossible for God to be glorified.

In the second place, Baxter's asks how a pastor can be successful when the pastor doesn't believe what he (or she) preaches. More than a concern for the honor of God as in the prior point, here Baxter is questioning the possibility for success when a pastor's heart is not genuinely called and committed. How can there be success when the pastor is not fully serious about what he is preaching, and cannot really preach with passion? How is it possible to be passionate about something one fails to really believe? "Sirs, do you think they will be heartily diligent to save men from hell, that be not heartily persuaded that there is a hell?"[65]

Next, in the form of a question, will one fight against Satan "who is himself a servant of Satan?"[66] Here is a vivid reminder that Baxter's primary concern in point 8 of section 2 is the danger of an unconverted ministry. Apparently, the subject in his mind is not a weak pastor, or even an outwardly sinning pastor, but the pastor who has never been regenerated. Even though these preachers may seem highly skilled, "it is all but an affected fervency."[67] It simply cannot make any rational sense, for "every unrenewed man is so far from hating sin to purpose, that it is his dearest treasure."[68]

Finally, the unconverted one who attempts to carry on pastoral ministry will inevitably be met by people who will not believe him (or her). "They will hardly believe a man that seemeth not to believe himself."[69]

---

64. Ibid., 80.
65. Ibid., 81.
66. Ibid., 82.
67. Ibid., 83.
68. Ibid., 84.
69. Ibid.

Baxter's work, now accepted as a classic of pastoral theology, places a tremendous weight of responsibility upon the pastor's shoulders and strongly underscores the demands that come with the office. But is there a connection between these heavy burdens and the criticisms of C. Fitzsimons Allison? It is Allison's contention that in the theology of Baxter, justifying faith includes obedience, thus the Christian contributes to some degree to his or her own justification.[70] Does the heavy responsibility Baxter describes reflect what Allison labels Baxter's "moralism?" To the degree his criticisms of Baxter (and others) are accurate, it would be logical to conclude that this moral impulse would carry over into his pastoral theology; thus, the pastor would bear the remarkable burden of making sure his or her congregants conduct their lives in strict Christian obedience. To fall short of this call would, in fact, expose people to the risk of hell itself.

Whether or not Allison's critiques are relevant in this regard, it remains true that Baxter presents an important historical example of this stress upon both the great demands and hazards inherent in pastoral ministry. Thus, Purves comments that *The Reformed Pastor* is a fresh voice in view of today's psychologically-oriented approach to pastoral care: "Much has changed since Baxter's day, but not the connivance and duplicity of the human heart, nor the seductions to which ministers are especially exposed."[71] In view of this, and in view of a seeming lack of voices willing to deal head-on with this "connivance and duplicity," indeed Baxter's words are important to heed.

---

70. C. Fitzsimons Allison, *The Rise of Moralism* (Vancouver: Regent College Publishing, 2003), 163.

71 Purves, 107.

Chapter 7

Gilbert Burnet

How much holier ought the priests of this religion to be.

GILBERT BURNET WAS A near contemporary of Richard Baxter. Although Baxter was English and Burnet, Scottish, both served the same Church of England and suffered their own trials directly related to changes on the political landscape. Born September 18, 1643 as the eleventh child of Robert Burnet, Gilbert clearly had a happy childhood, later commenting that his father was "one of the best fathers that ever a man was blessed with."[1] After studying at both Cambridge and Oxford, Burnet became minister of the parish in Saltoun, some fifteen miles from Edinburgh, at just twenty-one years old. His ordination came on June 15, 1665.

At Saltoun he was consumed with the busy work of pastoral ministry. Three times a week he preached and catechized the young and old. He paid pastoral visits to each house twice a year, and visited the sick each day. Later, he would confess that in these early years he labored under "a load of self-conceit and vanity."[2] Nevertheless, he found himself in some controversy with the publication of his *Memorial of Diverse Grievances*, which attacked the clergy and bishops for the low moral state of Scotland. This nearly led to his excommunication.[3]

---

1. T. E. S. Clarke and H. C. Foxcroft, *A Life of Gilbert Burnet* (Cambridge: The University Press, 1907), 21.

2. Ibid., 55.

3. J. D. Douglas, "Burnet, Gilbert" in *The New International Dictionary of the Christian*

After five years labor in the Anglican parish of Saltoun, Burnet was offered the position of Professor of Divinity at Glasgow, which he served with distinction for four and a half years, at which time he became Professor of Theology. Here he stood out for his industry. "His great learning, his tireless industry, his religious enthusiasm, and, it may be added, his complacent self-confidence made Burnet an admirable teacher."[4]

It was here, however, hoping for theological toleration, that Burnet ran into trouble. "His moderation in an age of extremes . . . was resented by both Presbyterian and Episcopalian parties . . . ."[5] The situation became so tense that he resigned his professorship at age thirty-one and came to London as rector of the Chapel of the Rolls and lecturer at St. Clements. The year was 1675. In London, Burnet came into favor with Charles II, but was later banned over his collision with the Duke of Lauderdale. The situation only worsened when he was dismissed by James II and driven into exile on the continent. That exile was the beginning of a new phase in Burnet's life. In Holland he was summoned to the court of William of Orange where he began to provide advice, especially to Mary, who he served as chaplain and advisor. Hearing of Burnet's influence on the hopeful monarchs, James tried to lure Burnet back to England to try him for treason, but to no avail. Thus, when James was driven into exile, Burnet returned with the new monarchs and their army to deliver their coronation sermon and continue in royal service as chaplain. Later he would be consecrated Bishop of Salisbury.

It is Burnet's shifting of opinion that has caught the attention of recent scholarship.[6] Early in his career, Burnet made clear his opinion that the king had the right to change church government and make alterations to certain matters of faith, and the people have no right resist. Ironically, Burnet later became one of William III's staunchest supporters in his overthrow of James II. According to Gibson, his views changed for two reasons.[7] First, Burnet came to believe that ultimately the rights of self-defense and self-preservation trump a king's aggressive schemes. Secondly, a madman, even a royal madman, would have to be stopped.

Church, ed. JD Douglas (Grand Rapids: Zondervan, 1978), 169.

4. Clarke and Foxcroft, 82.

5. J. D. Douglas, 169.

6. Robert Cornwall, *Gilbert Burnet's Discourse of the Pastoral Care* (Lewiston: Edwin Mellen Press, 1997), 12, See also William Gibson, *The Church of England, 1688–1822: Unity and Accord* (London: Routledge, 2001), 28.

7. Gibson, 8.

So Gibson concludes, "From this it was a short stop to his justification of William's mission."[8]

Even the *Discourse* itself emerged out of political and ecclesiastical struggles. Queen Mary asked him to write the work out of her own concern for the state of the English church. Furthermore, Burnet was a Latitudinarian, firmly believing in tolerance over issues of minor theological significance. John Gascoigne explains that "Burnet believed that one should allow a degree of latitude in matters of indifference."[9] In fact, evidence of this latitude appears in the *Discourse* as he suggests books for pastors according to their particular theological perspective. So he recommends an Arminian book for those so inclined, and a Calvinist theological work for others.[10] Thus, Robert Cornwall suggests that this very approach feeds the purpose of the *Discourse*: "It was intended to explain how a state-established church tried to cope pastorally with the newly passed Act of Toleration."[11] If for no other reason, now the State church had to confront the reality that it had competition, as it were, and it needed an increasingly sharp clergy. In some sense then, Burnet's work was written to address political and religious changes.

Despite his Latitudinarian inclinations, Burnet cannot be accused, as were others of like mind, of being liberal or even moderate in theological convictions. What Burnet produced in his *Discourse* "was a rigorous, demanding and aspirational ideology, requiring extraordinary dedication and commitment by both the clergy and laity."[12] It is this rigor, coupled with great energy and zeal that characterized Burnet's life and marks his *Discourse*.

Burnet brought his distinctive energy to the bishop's task, but clearly brought a pastor's love for the flock. After his appointment, Burnet immediately began a systematic visitation program throughout his diocese, extending pastoral care to those in need. From his own diary: "I stay a week in a place, where every morning I go and preach and confirm in some church within six or seven miles of the place, and then at five o'clock after evening prayer I catechize some children, and explain the whole

---

8. Ibid.

9. John Cascoigne, *Cambridge in the Age of the Enlightenment* (Cambridge: Cambridge University Press, 1989), 40.

10. Gilbert Burnet, *A Discourse of the Pastoral Care* (1692), x.

11. Cornwall, 2.

12. Gibson, 52.

Catechism to them, so that I go through it all in six days and confirm there next Lord's Day . . . and I have them dine with me in the Lord's day. This seems to be the most profitable method I can devise both for instructing, as well as provoking, the clergy to catechize much, and for setting a good emulation among the younger sort to be instructed."[13]

A DISCOURSE OF THE PASTORAL CARE

The diary entry quoted above provides an excellent backdrop by which to survey *A Discourse of the Pastoral Care,* for it is partly a description of this ministry he modeled. In fact, Burnet was one who strongly believed in setting an example for his clergy to follow. Before we survey this document, it should be mentioned that Burnet was a prolific writer. The bibliography in Clarke and Foxcroft's definitive biography covers thirty-four pages! Nevertheless, *A Discourse* represents a document he "preferred to his other writings."[14]

As we have seen, *A Discourse* comes alive when it is seen against the backdrop of Burnet's ministry as Bishop, and when it is held up to the larger historical setting of the English church. Burnet's *Discourse* was written in 1692 after Queen Mary of Orange urged him to write it out of a concern for the state of English clergy. In the book itself, Burnet regularly refers to the English Reformation, and contends that it has not firmly rooted itself; indeed, the Reformation is not really complete. In fact, the Reformation, by then some 150 years old, had been recently suffering setbacks according to Burnet.[15] It is Burnet's interpretation of the roots of this setback that is most unique. "The true reason of the slackning [sic] of the work, must be imputed to the Reformation made in several points with relation to the manners and labours of the clergy, *by the Church of Rome"* [italics mine].[16] In Burnet's view, since the Council of Trent (1545–1563), Roman Catholic theology had clearly differentiated itself from Protestant theology, but there were certain positive reforms that resulted among Roman clergy. He speaks of a certain new discipline among Roman clergy that should make Reformed clergy "ashamed."[17] Currently, Burnet observes, Roman parish

13. Clarke & Foxcroft, 290, 291.
14. Ibid., 310.
15. Burnet, x.
16. Ibid.
17. Ibid., xi.

priests are carrying out their duty with exemplary success, to the degree that "the parish priests have almost universally recovered the esteem of the people."[18] What has simultaneously transpired, in Burnet's view, is that the Reformed movement has basked in the protection and encouragement of princes and states which has led them to slack off in their zeal. So, while "popery" has purified itself from former abuses, Reformed clergy have added new ones! Here Burnet mentions a lessening in pastoral care, weakened preaching, and failure in the study of the Scriptures. The most significant result, he contends, is that Reformed Catholic clergy, having backed away from these duties, have become consumed with the public performance of duty. "Thus the pastoral care, the instructing, the exhorting, the admonishing and reproving, the directing and conducting, the visiting and comforting the people of the parish, is generally neglected."[19] So, like Baxter argued nearly four decades before, the reason for this loss of Reformation ground is the clergy, "the depravation under which most of the Reformed churches are fallen."[20]

It appears that Burnet had solid reason for his concern over the state of the ministry, for the significance of his *Discourse* is illuminated even more when one observes its larger contemporary context. In a helpful work based on extensive research into seventeenth- and eighteenth-century religious life in England, Donald Spaeth brings to light the condition of the Protestant Churches and their clergy, much of which serves to confirm the gloomy portrait that Burnet paints in *A Discourse of the Pastoral Care*.[21]

Spaeth introduces his findings with a broad warning: "It is difficult to generalize about the clergy of the late seventeenth- and eighteenth-century England because individual experiences differed so greatly . . . There was no such thing as a 'typical' clergyman."[22] One of the findings the author makes is that there was a great disparity among clergy because there was a tremendous disparity in their incomes. "Since the late seventeenth century most observers have agreed that the great majority of . . . the parish clergy,

---

18. Ibid., xiii.

19. Ibid., xvi.

20. Ibid., x.

21. Donald A. Spaeth, *The Church in the Age of Danger: Parsons and Parishoners 1660–1740* in Cambridge Studies in Early Modern British History, eds. Anthony Fletcher, John Guy, and John Morrill (Cambridge: Cambridge University Press, 2000), 31.

22. Ibid.

lived in poverty."²³ It is Spaeth's contention that this poverty meant that few ministers could perform their work without an outside income, leading to the ineptitude, and sometimes misbehavior, of the English clergy.

Much of Spaeth's research is based upon the archives left from the "presentments" churchwardens made to the bishop once every three years reporting the state of clergy and people. Each parish, sometimes in consultation with the vicar, selected a churchwarden for this responsibility. The most shocking cases revealed in these presentments revolved around cases of scandalous behavior; much more common were "simple" cases of pastoral neglect. Apparently, these cases were quite common. In the deanery of Amesbury between 1662 and 1714, Spaeth notes that one in five churchwardens' presentments expressed dissatisfaction with their clergy. Between 1662 and 1750, 127 presentments were made against the clergy in Salisbury where Burnet served as bishop from 1689–1715, "Yet bishops continued to take particular care for the quality of the clergy, particularly under Burnet."²⁴ In fact, thirty-two of the ninety-eight questions the bishop addressed to churchwardens concerned the clergy.

The curious case of one William Durston took place under the bishopric of Burnet. Durston had been called as rector of Tockenham Wick in 1683, before Burnet's tenure as Bishop began. What began as a happy appointment did not last long, for Durston had another "living" (pastoral position) in Worcestershire where he was born. Traveling between the two posts, he spent only one day a week in Tockenham. In 1686, the churchwarden presented him to the bishop for failing to reside among them and not providing a curate (assistant). Durston immediately counter-attacked with charges that the wardens were neglecting the church facilities to the degree that the church tower was in danger of collapsing. This heated exchange did result in Tockenham getting a curate, but when the curate arrived, Durston virtually disappeared. By 1689, the present warden complained that the rector had not been seen for three years! Unfortunately, the curate left the parish in 1690, and two years later it was reported that Durston had visited this parish but once in the preceding six months. The residents of that community not only complained about Durston's negligence, they were upset over his quarrelsomeness, especially regarding money. He neglected to pay his parish clerk or the

23. Ibid.
24. Ibid., 114.

curate. Once, Durston avoided the tax collector by having the bells rung for service to begin while he ditched into the alehouse to hide. The situation only worsened as some parishioners, in an act of defiance, threw stones through the windows of the church and blamed it on the wind. Not least among his problems was that Durston clearly had an issue with drinking. At one point, he was so drunk that he fell off his horse in front of a crowd. All in all, churchwardens presented Durston to the bishop and archdeacons four times in seven years.

Pluralism was a continual issue in Burnet's world. Pluralism referred to one pastor serving two parishes simultaneously. It was assumed, in that age of minimal travel, that the pastor would live in the village where he ministered; pluralism, of course, made that impossible. Thus, the complaint arose that an absent pastor could not possibly give proper pastoral attention to one's people. Spaeth, however, suggests that the practice of pluralism was economically driven; it was sometimes a priest's only means of producing a sustainable income. In some situations where the clergyman could effectively carry out dual "livings," pluralism was tolerated. In many cases, however, the practice led to pastoral neglect. Unless the incumbent took measures to supply a curate in his place, pluralism made it virtually impossible for him to read the divine service twice on Sundays and to fulfill pastoral duties during the week.[25]

This kind of neglect is precisely the concern of Burnet's *Discourse*. "It is chiefly on design to raise the sense of the obligations of the clergy to the duties of the pastoral care, that this book is written."[26] So his book "was therefore written to recall his clergy to their true profession . . . The mere fact that Burnet felt that he needed to write his book suggests that his ideal of pastoral ministry was far from universal in the Church of England."[27] In the words of Clark and Foxcroft: "Simple, fervent, and sincere, the passionate solicitude of the author for the reform of the pastoral ideal lends force and unity to the whole. It points with pathetic intensity the supreme convictions of his life; and every sentence glows with an ardour of spiritual fire."[28]

---

25. Ibid., 115–16.

26. Burnet, xviii.

27. David Cornick, "Pastoral Care in England," in *A History of Pastoral Care*, ed. GR Evans (London: Cassell, 2000), 322.

28. Clarke and Foxcroft, 310.

Great was the influence of Burnet's *Discourse*. Burnet himself later thanked God that his work "had good effect on many persons."[29] Nevertheless, as with all great works, "It was criticized for exposing the defects of the Church to the nation, so clergymen may have been reluctant to turn to it for advice."[30] Of course, Burnet himself was a man under influence, and that source was none other than Richard Baxter, "to whom he had been recommended . . . and from whose books he had derived much benefit."[31]

Approaching his subject like a grand theological treatise, it appears Burnet intended his work to be exhaustive. In the end, he had produced a primer on pastoral theology. First, he treats the pastor's role by examining the titles used for the same throughout Scripture. Second, he gleans insight from the Old Testament patterns established for priests, followed, third, by relevant New Testament passages. His fourth section attempts to garner the early church's portrayal of the pastor, followed by subsequent historical insights. Sixth, he surveys the Church of England's attempts to raise the obligations of clergy higher than before. Burnet then shifts his attention, seventh, to how clergy should be formed. Eighth, he considers the public functions of clergy, and finally, he addresses the great task and responsibility of preaching. Burnet's work then, is a cry for faithful shepherds.

We begin by noticing that, like Gregory of Nazianzus before him, the call to pastoral ministry is a high and lofty calling. This can be seen in the many characteristics that "ought" to describe the pastor. He *ought* to be separated from the cares and concerns of the world. He *ought* to live his life as a pattern for others, offer prayers for them, distribute the Bread of Life among them, and reprove them. Indeed, Burnet's description of the pastor's vocation presents one with an intimidating charge: "He is to watch over their souls, to keep them from error, and to alarm them out of their sins, by giving them warning of the judgments of God; to visit the sick, and to prepare them for the judgment and the life to come."[32]

So clergy are under greater obligation than others by virtue of their call. Just as the priest of the Old Testament was set apart unto holiness, the pastor is called to exemplary purity. Thus, the preparation of priests

29. Ibid., 314.
30. Spaeth, 108–9.
31. Clarke and Foxcroft, 38.
32. Ibid., 3.

for ministry concerns two fundamental issues: First, cultivating a right temper and secondly, developing excellence in study.[33] Clearly, the former is priority. "We ought certainly to begin with our souls."[34] This starting point though, must not be underestimated, for the pastor "must break himself of the appetites of pleasure, or wealth, or ambition, or authority . . . ."[35] Again, the first demand outweighs the second: "A great measure of piety, with a very small proportion of learning, will carry one a great way . . . ."[36] That does not mean, however, that there is a lessened emphasis upon learning, for this too presents a great demand. Besides needing great familiarity with the Greek New Testament, Burnet spends a couple of pages recommending other contemporary resources with which one must be familiar. Nevertheless, even when the pastor has been properly prepared for the great responsibilities that lie ahead, he (or she) will still face various hazards that come simply by virtue of being in the ministry.

Like Baxter, Burnet, at the beginning of his work, references Acts 20.28, which represents a clarion call to watch over oneself. So, in the first section where he considers the various scriptural titles that describe the pastoral call, Burnet mentions "soldier," and then comments, "The fatigue, the dangers and difficulties of the state of life are so well understood, that no application is necessary to make them more sensible."[37] Just as no soldier carries out his duty without running tremendous bodily risks, no pastor carries out his without great spiritual risk.

Like so many early writers before him, Burnet is clear in stating that the pastor's exposure to judgment is greater than it is for others. Treating the Old Testament priesthood as a pattern for contemporary ministry, Burnet emphasizes the necessity of being set apart for fear of impending judgment. He then minces no words while making a reference to Eli's sons. If pastors fail to behave, "God will glorify himself by his severe judgments on them."[38] Again, employing very strong language, pastors "ought to consider themselves under very strict obligations, by that charge of which they must give a severe account at the great day, in which the

33. Ibid., 142.
34. Ibid., 156.
35. Ibid., 143.
36. Ibid., 165.
37. Ibid., 12.
38. Ibid., 17.

blood of all those who perished through their neglect and default, shall be required at their hands."[39] The language here is very reminiscent of the words of the church's earlier writers, so it is no surprise that Burnet, obviously well-read, begins a lengthy summary of Gregory of Nazianzus' Second Oration, a writer he calls "a great man."[40] In fact, citing Gregory extensively, his treatment of the Oration stretches to ten pages in the 1692 edition of his *Discourse*. Whether he was alerted to the concern of judgment by reading Gregory, or not, he certainly notices this earlier bishop's warnings about sure and certain judgment to befall any who fail in their duty. Sketching out the general contours of Gregory's biographical background to the Oration, he references Gregory's deep awareness of Ezekiel 34, which highlights the judgment of God on "bad priests."[41]

After he deals with Gregory, there comes another extensive treatment that runs ten pages, this time of Chrysostom's *Six Books on the Priesthood*. Here, Burnet launches into a variety of other hazards that are endemic to this ministry. From the beginning of his Chrysostom citations, Burnet calls attention to a repeated Chrysostom theme: The danger of losing one's own soul while caring for the souls of others. So he sets the stage: "To have both the powers of darkness, and the works of the flesh to fight against, required no ordinary measure both of strength and courage."[42] Like Gregory, Burnet mentions Chrysostom's concerns for purity and holiness; so much so, that priests must achieve a greater degree of it than another. This holiness is even more pronounced during Holy Eucharist, when "his thoughts should carry him heavenwards . . . how much holier ought the priests of this religion to be."[43]

So, reflecting on Chrysostom's work, Burnet asserts that this holy priest must go to great lengths to avoid ambition. Summarizing the *Six Books*, Burnet notes that those given to ambition are most of all exposed to temptations, gladly provoked by the failures of others, courting applause and fawning over great people. "Certainly a worthy priest has no ambitious aspirings."[44] It is one thing to desire the office of bishop when

---

39. Ibid., 28–29.
40. Ibid., 65.
41. Ibid.
42. Ibid., 67.
43. Ibid., 69.
44. Ibid., 70.

one considers the toil involved, but it is another when one wants it because of its power and authority, for these people can hardly rebuke sin. As is the case with any priestly fault, the same allowances are not made to pastors as to others because the world expects great things from them. The degree to which Burnet's interest in this issue is connected to the on-going problems associated with pluralism is unknown, but one can imagine that some amount of his passionate warning about ambition was fueled by this concern.

Moving forward from a treatment of historical writings, Burnet becomes the first of the writers considered here to clearly identify the warnings about pastoral ministry spelled out in the *Book of Common Prayer*. This constitutes his concern in chapter six. To begin with, Burnet contends that the Church of England intended to raise the standards of pastoral ministry higher than before; although, as we noted earlier, the state of the pastoral ministry was at a current low. Building on the premise that the truest heart of a Church is found in her official language,[45] he moves on, in succession, to review the language employed at the ordination of a deacon, a priest, and a bishop. In the case of the priest, Burnet notes how the figures of the watchman, shepherd, and steward are employed in the rites of the *Book of Common Prayer*, followed by "the greatness of the fault of their negligence, and the horrible punishment that will follow upon it . . . ."[46] In fact, the 1662 edition of the *Book of Common Prayer* articulates these hazards quite plainly. "Have always therefore printed in your remembrance, how great a treasure is committed to your charge. For they are the sheep of Christ, which he bought with his death, and for whom he shed his blood. The Church and Congregation whom you must serve, is his Spouse, and his Body. And if it shall happen that the same Church, or any Member thereof, do take any hurt or hindrance by reason of your negligence, ye know the greatness of the fault, and also the horrible punishment that will ensue."[47]

Finally, there are other spiritual hazards that one faces by virtue of being in pastoral ministry. For instance, Burnet warns that the pastor's life and example can bring ruin to others, thus heaping on himself eternal ruin. "If he perishes, he does not perish alone, but carries a Shoal down

45. Ibid., 104.
46. Ibid., 115.
47. *Book of Common Prayer of the Church of England*, 1662. Ordinal, "Ordering of Priests."

with him, either of those who have perished in ignorance, through his neglect; or those who have been hardened in their souls by his example: and since all this must be put to his account, it may be justly inferred from hence, that no man can have a heavier share in the miseries of another State than profane and wicked clerks."[48] The responsibility to be an example to others carries with it a heavy toll when failure happens, for "a priest therefore is more accountable to God, and the world for his deportment and will be more severely accounted with than any other person whatsoever. He is more watched over and observed than all others . . . ."[49]

Although not treating the hazards of ministry as exhaustively or as orderly as does Baxter, Burnet has clearly identified several reasons for the pastor to pause and consider the risks of ministry to his or her own soul. Further, seen against the background of the historical context, it takes little imagination to appreciate the lengths to which Burnet was willing to go to warn his pastors of the consequences of pastoral neglect. His burden to more fully establish the Reformation in England is clearly sensed in the pages of his *Discourse*. It is also little wonder, given the historical setting, that Burnet's work "had good effect on many persons."[50]

---

48. Ibid., 147–48.
49. Ibid., 177.
50. Clarke and Foxcroft, 314.

CHAPTER 8

George Bull

Every teacher is accountable for the souls committed to his charge.

GEORGE BULL, THE BISHOP of St. Davids, Wales, has much to offer us regarding the topic of our concern. Born in Somerset County as an only child, Bull's mother tragically died when he was only four. His early education was classical, after which he matriculated into Exeter College, Oxford. Despite coming of age during the Commonwealth, Bull refused to take an oath to it, thus indicating his political and ecclesiastical leanings. What makes his refusal even more curious is that his early years were spent studying with the noted divine, William Thomas, who "was always reckoned a puritan."[1] The tensions characterizing this period resulted in his being ordained the same day he applied for ordination in 1655 by the ousted Anglican Oxford bishop Robert Skinner.[2] Considering the influence of Thomas, it would make eminent sense for Bull's theology to have a tone of Puritanism in it. However, as with his contemporary Richard Baxter, C. Fitzsimons Allison takes Bull to task for departing from the classical Anglican (and Reformed) theology of Richard Hooker.[3] Focusing on Bull's *Harmonia Apostolica* (1670), Allison analyzes the

---

1. Robert Nelson, "The Life of Bishop Bull," in *The Works of George Bull, DD, Lord Bishop of St. David's*, ed. Rev. Edward Burton, DD (1846), 19.

2. Robert D. Cornwall, "Bull, George (1634–1710)," in *Oxford Dictionary of National Biography*, ed. H. C. G. Matthew and Brian Harrison (Oxford: OUP, 2004), http://www.oxforddnb.com/view/article/3903 (accessed August 12, 2008).

3. Allison, 118ff.

comparison Bull makes between Paul's doctrine of justification by faith and James' emphasis on works. It is here, Allison argues, that Bull strays from classical theology by insisting that the elect are not merely justified by their faith, but by their works. So, Allison points out the divergence of Bull's theology: "Thus it follows that because we are justified by our faith and repentance, and because both faith and repentance include works, we are, in fact, justified by works."[4] He continues by noting certain charges made against Bull in his day, as well as many published refutations of his theology. In the end, Allison concludes: "He must be placed with Taylor, Thorndike, and Hammond in the vanguard of what was to become the predominant school of Anglican moralism."[5]

Regardless of his theological leanings, Bull's ministry, which began at St. George's near Bristol, was always distinguished by his great learning. He faithfully spent two months each year at the libraries of Oxford, making extensive use of the original languages. "To say the truth, Mr. Bull's chief delight was in his books, and his study was the scene of his most exquisite pleasure . . . ."[6] After his marriage to Bridget Gregory on May 20, 1658, Bull became rector of St. Mary. His marriage would grow fruit as would his ministry; eventually Bull fathered five sons and six daughters. Before his elevation to bishop, for twenty-seven years, Bull was pastor of St. Peter's at Suddington where he preached twice on Sundays and showed great faithfulness in both private and family devotions. It was at Suddington where Bull found himself privy to the plans for restoration and even hosted a meeting of conspirators intending to overthrow Cromwell and his cronies. Finally, after the ups and downs of the pro-Catholic reigns of Charles and his brother, and after the Glorious Revolution, Bull found favor. In 1701, he was appointed bishop of St. David's in his advanced years. After a lengthy illness, with a final "amen" to a prayer said on his behalf, Bull died on February 17, 1710.

During his effective life and ministry, Bull also produced a number of books in Latin, beginning with the aforementioned *Harmonia Apotolica*. He even lived to see an edition of his Latin works published in 1703. Apart from these writings, only accessible to the educated of his day, scores of Bull's sermons and discourses were published, including

---

4. Ibid., 119.
5. Ibid., 136.
6. Ibid., 76.

his visitation sermon, the subject of our present concern. The sermon, formally titled, "A Visitation Sermon Concerning the Great Difficulty and Danger of the Priestly Ministry," was preached to the clergy of St. David's in 1708, just two years before his death. In the sermon, Bull lays out four qualities necessary for the clergy of his day: knowledge, prudence, exemplary holiness, and responsibility for one's parishioners. Along with the qualities come five duties: reading services, preaching, catechizing, administering communion, and visiting the sick. Beyond that, however, the sermon clearly reflects a concern over the 1689 Toleration Act by William and Mary, which created a sort of competition between independents and Anglicans. So, as Gibson puts it, "The new environment of Toleration demanded renewed efforts by the clergy."[7] Thus, it very much appears that in addition to identifying pastoral qualities and duties, Bull also wanted parishioners to know how highly trained *their* clergy were, while taking a stab at dissenters: "How horrible is the confidence, or rather impudence, of those mechanicks, [sic] that have leaped from the shopboard or plough into the pulpit, and thus, *per saltum*, by a prodigious leap, commenced teachers! . . . 'Tis a miracle, that any such person should dare to preach; or, if he do, that any man, in his right wits, should vouchsafe to hear him."[8]

A VISITATION SERMON

Characteristic of his studious nature, Bull begins his visitation sermon by observing the fact that the first verse of James 3 has been variously interpreted: "My brethren, be not many masters, knowing that we shall receive the greater condemnation." Despite his demonstrated capacity for technical debates involving the original languages, Bull swiftly moves to his interpretation. The text is a "caution against the rash undertaking of the pastoral office."[9] This office implores caution because of its dangers, and its dangers can be identified along with the duties that come with pastoral ministry. The office requires a great amount of knowledge, prudence, and holiness.

The endeavors of ministry also demand knowledge. Here Bull demonstrates a familiarity with Gregory of Nazianzus. Quoting Gregory, Bull

---

7. William Gibson, *The Church of England, 1688–1822: Unity and Accord* (London: Routledge, 2001), 213.

8. George Bull, "A Visitation Sermon Concerning the Great Difficulties and Danger of the Priestly Office" in *A Companion for the Candidates for Holy Orders* (1794), 38–39.

9. Bull, 6.

believes that theology is the art of arts and science of sciences; however, its endeavor also demands great knowledge, which requires no small effort. In fact, employing a metaphor, "He must keep a table well furnished with these heavenly provisions for all comers."[10] Bull then devotes energy to breaking down the various areas of knowledge a minister must have in order to succeed. Like a grammarian must be aware of the elements of grammar, a minister must be versed in the basics of Christian theology. Then he must be able to defend the faith, thus providing security for his sheep. Furthermore, he must be a practical "physician" who is well-versed in casuistry, able to assuage doubt and tackle difficult cases. Turning to the Scriptures themselves, he urges his preachers to be like Apollos in Acts 18.24: "Mighty in the Scriptures."

To knowledge, Bull adds prudence and wisdom, although this section takes up much less space in the printed sermon. Here he speaks of "wisdom in the soul that animates and enlivens knowledge."[11] The issue that the minister deals with is no less than the eternal salvation of his people's souls, which requires tremendous wisdom in preaching, in carrying himself (or herself), in common conversation, in the governance of his (or her) family, and in caring for the flock.

Third, knowledge and wisdom are not enough, for the pastoral ministry demands tremendous holiness, which Bull calls "an exemplary holiness."[12] Here, Bull begins by comparison. Knowledge is requisite for the pastor's office, but knowledge is clearly not enough, for knowledgeable men are a blessing, but sinful men of great knowledge are an abomination. He explains: "Learned and knowing men, of ill lives, have been always the greatest stumbling block in the Church of God, but attended with the ruin of many others . . . ."[13] No knowledgeable person who is sinful, sins alone. The bishop is here very careful and does not mince words: "He is the greatest and most desperate sinner."[14] As a brilliant and learned man himself, Bull was keenly aware that any guilty person with great knowledge "doubtless increases his guilt."[15] These are people who "daily behold the wonders

10. Ibid., 14.
11. Ibid., 32.
12. Ibid., 26.
13. Ibid., 28.
14. Ibid., 29.
15. Ibid., 30.

of the Lord and daily converseth in the great depth of the holy Scriptures."[16] Clearly, knowledge accompanied by sin is an issue of the heart.

Referring to knowledge, prudence, and holiness as difficulties and dangers of pastoral duty,[17] Bull then seems to add another. "Every teacher is accountable for the souls committed to his charge."[18] Here it becomes clear that Bull was familiar with the ancient writings considered earlier. Employing a quotation straight from the Greek text of Chrysostom's *De Sacerdotio*, Bull seems to empathize with the writer who confesses that considering the office of priest leaves him shaking.[19] In Chrysostom's words: "The fear of this threat continually disturbs my spirit."[20] Noting Hebrews 13.17 in this context, which states that leaders must give account for the souls in their care, Bull makes extensive use of Chrysostom's commentary on Hebrews, and concludes, "He must be a man of very firm shoulders, that is not crushed under it [the weight of the burden]."[21]

Not unlike Burnet, who wrote shortly before Bull's sermon was delivered, Bull shows a familiarity with, and commitment to, the rites of ordination in the Church of England. In fact, Bull's citation of the ordination rite is exactly the same as Burnet's.[22] Imploring his fellow pastors, the bishop urges his listeners to go to whatever length is necessary to escape the judgment sure to come on those negligent in their duty.

George Bull ends his sermon in a unique way, thus making a distinct contribution to our study. At the end, he addresses the people under his listeners' care. In short, based on the awareness that each priest is in danger by virtue of being in pastoral ministry, Bull "turns the tables" by suggesting that the members of the flock themselves are not immune from danger. Admitting that it is a miracle that anyone would dare enter into the pulpit, the hearer must be equally afraid, for to listen exposes one to truth, a truth for which one becomes accountable. With this, Bull reminds the parishioner that while the pastor must answer for the souls of his (or her) people, it is the people's souls themselves that are in danger

16. Ibid, 30–31.
17. Ibid., 32.
18. Ibid.
19. Ibid.
20. John Chrysostom, *De Sacerdotio* (AD 391), 6.1.
21. Bull, 34.
22. Ibid., 35. See *Book of Common Prayer of the Church of England*, 1662. Ordinal, "Ordering of Priests."

from this negligence. "'Tis the danger your own souls are in . . . if not carefully looked to, that is the great hazard of our office . . . what need have you to look to yourselves."[23] Yes, the pastor bears much weight, but while he or she must answer to God for the souls of their flock, the people must remember that it is their souls that are at risk.

Even at the very end of the sermon, Bull has something different to offer. Given the risk inherent to the pastor's office, a risk of his eternal soul, he includes himself and urges the flock "to pity us, to pray for us, to encourage us, by all possible ways and means . . . ."[24] Not content to leave the burden entirely with his pastors, Bull recognizes individual responsibility and distributes it evenly.

---

23. Ibid., 39.
24. Ibid.

Chapter 9

William Paley

*Pastors must prepare themselves for dangers,
to which they are, more than commonly, exposed.*

WILLIAM PALEY'S 1795 SERMON is the final document under our consideration. It is the final document, not simply because it is dated last, but because it represents a certain development in thinking regarding the issue of our concern. No doubt, this development is due to the Enlightenment, which Immanuel Kant explained with his watchword: "Have the courage to make use of your own understanding."[1] This anthropological emergence into adulthood meant that guidance from someone else was no longer necessary; human beings were pronounced capable of thinking and reasoning for themselves, as opposed to blindly accepting what had been passed down as definitive truth. This pursuit of reason is exemplified in "Dangers Incidental to the Clerical Character," for in it, Paley demonstrates a transition from our previous authors' attempts to merely identify and explain the spiritual hazards of ministry, to searching for the root causes behind them. Paley's contribution to our topic then, brings us to a new level of inquiry.

A brief four years after his death, the Quarterly Review wrote the following about the late Reverend William Paley: "No modern writer perhaps has diffused more widely the knowledge of moral and religious truth. None has seen his works pass through more editions in the same

---

1. Immanuel Kant, *Practical Philosophy*, trans. and ed. Mary J. Gregor (Cambridge: Cambridge University Press, 1996), 63.

time: and none will be found with more certainty to hold a place on the shelf of every private library."[2]

Born in July of 1743, Paley's childhood and youth were marked by an insatiable curiosity. His father was a schoolmaster, so with education in his blood, Paley headed to Christ's College, Cambridge at sixteen years old. Upon graduation, he took a position as second assistant, teaching in a private school in Greenwich, but was quickly dissatisfied, desiring ordination instead. Too young yet to be ordained, he would have to wait until February 23, 1766. Chosen in the meantime as a fellow at Cambridge and tutor at Christ's College, Paley headed back to the venerable institution. In short, "Paley was eminently successful in his work at Christ's."[3] It seems that his classes were always full and he was popular as a private tutor. Whether or not his penchant for sneaking off to a local fishing hole to indulge his favorite recreational activity made him more popular with the students or not, is unknown. In fact, he may have been a Cambridge don who was also the stuff of caricature, for it was a popular joke that the rather uncoordinated Paley could barely stay on horseback, which was why he was scarcely to be found in the saddle.

It was never Paley's intention to stay at Cambridge long-term, so when he was offered a "living" at Great Musgrave in the Diocese of Carlisle, Paley relished the opportunity to serve as a country parson. It was at Great Musgrave that he met Jane Hewitt, whom he married on June 6, 1776. From there, Paley and his wife were off to St. Laurence parish in nearby Appleby, at which time he also took on the vicarage at Dalston. After meaningful service in these parishes, Paley and his family shifted his ministry focus on Stanwix, beginning in 1793. Sadly, Paley would not take this charge with his wife at his side, for in 1791, at age forty, she died, leaving Paley with the surviving eight of their ten children.

Not much is known about the details of his ministry; suffice it to say, his biographer described Paley as an "impressive preacher."[4] Preaching, however, was not his only charge, for it was during his time at Stanwix that Paley became involved in the work of the larger diocese by first serving as archdeacon, and later as chancellor to the bishop. Significant to our present concern, these roles involved him in issues of clergy discipline, among

---

2. M. L. Clarke, preface to *Paley: Evidences for the Man* (Toronto: University of Toronto Press, 1974).

3. Ibid., 27.

4. Ibid., 34.

other activities. He also became embroiled in the intense wrangling that led, with his help, to the abolition of the slave trade. Besides all of this, Paley busied himself reading, taking detailed notes, and writing. Somehow in the midst of this, Paley found love again, marrying Catherine Dobson in 1795, the same year he moved to Cambridge for his Doctor of Divinity degree.

William Paley's bright mind and discipline resulted in the production of a number of books, articles, and sermons, his final book being *Natural Theology*, published in 1802. Despite his productive ministry, however, it has been suggested that Paley was not popular with everyone. Robert Hole argues that Paley was at the "extreme 'liberal' end of the Anglican spectrum" both intellectually and theologically, with Unitarian leanings,[5] to the degree that evangelicals were his "bitterest critics" to the end.[6]

On the one hand, the Evangelical movement in England was tied to the incredible influence of John and Charles Wesley; on the other hand, it was a revival within the Church of England, distinct from the Wesleyan movement.[7] This Anglican revival tended to be Calvinistic according to Gordon Wakefield, and was associated with the likes of Charles Simeon, William Wilberforce, John Newton, and George Whitefield.[8] It was marked by the centrality of Scripture, conversion, a high regard for moral responsibility, world missions, and social reform. Herein lay the conflict. It is reported that Paley's theological convictions were a "late flowering" of the latitudinarian tradition, which did not match well with the convictions of the Evangelicals.[9] Furthermore, it is alleged that his intellectual curiosity got him into trouble since he seemed to have doubts about hell's eternity, and even tended to see the church as merely an ethical institution.[10] In short, "He combined a remarkable open-mindedness with a reluctance to disturb the peace of the Church."[11]

---

5. Robert Hole, *Pulpits, Politics, and Public Order in England: 1760–1832* (Cambridge: University of Cambridge Press, 1989), 79.

6. Ibid., 81.

7. Gordon S. Wakefield, "Anglican Spirituality," in *Christian Spirituality 3: Post Reformation and Modern*, ed. Louise Dupre and Don E. Saliers, (New York: Crossroad, 1991), 274.

8. Ibid.

9. John Cascoigne, *Cambridge in the Age of the Enlightenment* (Cambridge: Cambridge University Press, 1989), 239.

10. Ibid., 241.

11. Ibid.

Although settling this debate is not essential to our purpose, it is important to note that this common perspective on Paley has been questioned recently by A. M. C. Waterman.[12] Acknowledging that this characterization of Paley is found as early as 1906, Waterman nevertheless calls it "naïve," and suggests that Paley and his school enjoyed "increasingly conservative convictions."[13] In fact, Paley and his peers struck a *via media* between those who were blindly beholden to certain systems of theological thought and those who showed complete indifference to such systems. In this way, Waterman argues, Paley landed on a more conservative side than is usually alleged.

Wherever Paley stood on the eighteenth-century English theological spectrum, this much is certain: he had tremendous concerns regarding the spiritual dangers inherent in pastoral ministry. Such concerns are abundantly evident in his "Dangers Incidental to the Clerical Character" (1766), a sermon later published in book form. In short, the sermon focuses on six reasons why pastors are spiritually endangered by the process of conducting the affairs of ministry.

DANGERS INCIDENTAL

In this sermon, first printed in 1795, Paley directly addresses the issues that concern us. His title conveys his agenda: There are certain dangers that accompany pastoral ministry. Addressing the academic clergy at Cambridge, "He spoke of the more subtle dangers and temptations of the clerical profession."[14] Similar to the other writings under consideration, Paley bases his sermon on a specific text. In Paley's case, he calls upon 1 Corinthians 9.27: "Lest that, by any means, when I have preached to others, I myself should be a cast-away." The theme he trumpets is clearly portrayed. Nothing "will compensate for the neglect of personal self-government."[15] The problem with a lack of self-government is one that all humans face by their very nature, but it is an issue that is particularly difficult for those in pastoral ministry who "must prepare themselves for dangers, to which they are, more than commonly, exposed."[16]

12. A. M. C. Waterman, "A Cambridge 'Via Media' in Late Georgian Anglicanism," *Journal of Ecclesiastical History* 42, no. 3 (July 1991): 419.

13. Ibid., 420, 424.

14. Clarke, 118.

15. William Paley, *Dangers Incidental to the Clerical Character* (1795), 8.

16. Ibid., 9.

In the course of Paley's sermon, he progresses through six individual points to establish his claim. Each explains his initial assertion that there are "dangers adhering to the very nature of our profession."[17] It is important that the reader of Paley's sermon be aware that his approach is different than those already considered, because it is Paley's desire to dig out the "why" behind this reality. Apparently to Paley, noting the *causes* of the danger will supply the pastor with greater resolve and the acumen necessary to overcome these dangers.

Paley begins by purporting that by its very nature, the pastoral ministry creates an "insensibility to religious impression."[18] The simple fact here is that the pastor is constantly exposed to religious, or spiritual, truths, and this exposure creates a certain insensibility to the full significance of it. More particularly, when the pastor is engaged in *passively* repeating these great spiritual truths, the pastor hardens himself or herself to these truths. Paley's idea is that when one is actively engaged in something that is repeated, it strengthens the person, but if one is passively disengaged, he or she risks becoming hardened to it. A clergyman, Paley explains, "habitually conversant with the offices of religion, will be less moved and stimulated . . . ."[19] This phenomenon easily results in deadness to the thing being passed on in the same way that a person who is constantly exposed to something horrible will become accustomed to it. Paley provides an illustration of this by suggesting that regular exposure to trauma will harden a person, which he admits, may be good in some circumstances. In pastoral work, however, becoming hardened to the "religious impression" results in nothing positive. This is a reality, Paley preaches, that must be acknowledged and fiercely combated.

The second reality that Paley points to is the "unusual effort" that is required to bring one's studied conclusions back to oneself. It is, of course, the natural intention of the pastor to produce fruit in the lives of those he serves. Each pastor wants to produce effect, but one must beware, for "in philosophy itself, it is not always the same thing, to study a subject, in order to understand, and in order only to teach it."[20] It is altogether too easy for the pastor to care so much that the message have effect in the lives of

17. Ibid., 13.
18. Ibid., 9.
19. Ibid., 11.
20. Ibid., 12–13.

the parishioner, that the same pastor fails to apply the message to himself, or herself. "The secret duty, of turning truly and in earnest their attention upon themselves, is suspended, not say forgotten, amidst the labours, the engagements, the popularity of their public ministry...."[21]

Next, Paley expresses concern over the way clergy communicate themselves. "In our wishes to convince, we are extremely apt to overstate our arguments."[22] The zeal for communicating effectively, connected to the zeal for fruitful labor, may result in exaggeration in order to establish a point. The problem with this zeal, Paley argues, is that it defeats itself by destroying the power and influence of the argument on the one making it. This tendency to overstate for effect will eventually backfire on the pastor, for "it always destroys the efficacy of the argument upon ourselves."[23] The pastor knows the exaggeration, and is himself or herself corrupted by it. Furthermore, this practice weakens the pastor's ability to judge, for when the pastor consciously overstates, he or she eventually becomes convinced, and loses the perspective necessary to make sound judgments.

A fourth danger is identified as "literary trifling" which "has a tendency, above all other employments, to harden the heart."[24] One of the pastor's great privileges is to study the Scriptures in-depth, employing the tools necessary for gaining a solid understanding of the Holy Scriptures. This study is well and good; in fact, it is necessary. It is also dangerous, because the text of Scripture is meant not only to be studied, but obeyed. Clarke summarizes Paley's point: "If the book is of sufficient importance to deserve our study it ought to command our obedience."[25]

There arises a fifth concern that is related to the first four. Paley warns that a danger arises when one lives a life of great contemplation, and fails to live an active life. Paley confesses that this issue does not apply to the clergy as directly as it applies to those who live a contemplative life, but his warning is noteworthy: "It is difficult to sustain virtue by meditation alone."[26] The challenge the contemplative faces is that the conclusions one reaches cannot be firmly fixed or even formed unless those conclusions

---

21. Ibid., 13.
22. Ibid.
23. Ibid.
24. Ibid., 14.
25. Clarke, 119.
26. Paley, 17.

are challenged and tested in the fires of real life. Paley is merely identifying the reality that one cannot change and grow apart from the forces that come with living a full and engaged life. To withdraw from the common world, according to Paley, is to be deprived of the opportunity to apply studied hypotheses to real life.

The final issue that Paley surfaces is another danger that is directly connected to the rest. The pastor is in grave spiritual danger when the duty is performed solely for the sake of setting an example. When the pastor carries out the pastoral function based *solely* on the conviction that he or she is to provide an example, that pastor is in danger. "Whenever this is the case, it becomes not only a cold and extraneous, but a false and unreasonable principle of action."[27] Paley is very clear: "There must be some reason for every duty beside example, or there can be no sufficient reason for it at all."[28] His logic is rather simple. If the *only* reason one engages in a certain act is to set an example, there must be no virtue in the act alone, or else the action would be motivated by something other than setting an example. To be sure, setting an example is right and good, but it must "attend upon, not supersede, the proper motive of the action."[29] Paley may be at his best as he identifies the answer to the next logical question, what should be our motive? "The love of God; the zeal for his honor and service, which love, which gratitude, which piety inspires, are still to be the operating motive of your conduct."[30]

Indeed, Paley has offered us a unique perspective. His interest is not just in observing that there are dangers inherent to pastoral ministry, or even to remain satisfied with explaining those. Paley is concerned with understanding why pastors are uniquely exposed to these dangers. Instead of simply affirming the obvious, that pastors face temptation, or that they must deal with pride, Paley's desire has been to identify why these dangers exist in the first place. It is by obtaining knowledge of the roots of these dangers, Paley suggests, that those in pastoral ministry will be best served.

27. Ibid., 18.
28. Ibid.
29. Ibid., 19.
30. Ibid.

Part Three

Looking for Solutions

Chapter 10

Remedies from the Pastoral Theologians

Upon a closer reading of the pastoral literature from this period, one finds that these compositions were not entirely dire warnings. Clearly sensing the need for good balance and practical advice on how to avoid the dangers, the same writers also offer significant advice on overcoming, which usually amounts to exhortations about forming good habits. Good habits, these writers argue, must characterize the pastor's life in order to experience victory over the dangers that lurk in following so great a call.

We now turn our attention to identifying some of these habits and the writers who so passionately urged their implementation in the hope of creating what they might have called a more "godly and useful" clergy. A second purpose will be to take note of the diversity of religious and political convictions represented by these English authors, yet their amazingly unified voice when it came to their pastoral advice. Acknowledging the homogeneity among them, such as their common gender, their geographical location, and their historical period, it is nevertheless essential to note that many of these authors were at tremendous odds with each other both theologically and politically. Within their world, they represented great variety. We will see that although the political and ecclesiastical convictions among these writers vary greatly within the restrictions of their common setting, their pastoral theology is nearly uniform. It will be argued here that this uniformity creates a kind of timelessness to their advice.

In this final section, additional writers will be introduced, since the question over how to face the hazards of ministry necessitates hearing from writers other than those we have already considered. While some of the pastoral writers in the section to follow we have already met, we must become familiar with the others since their diverse biographies serve to underscore the power of their unified message.

ISAAC WATTS

Isaac Watts, most famous as a hymn writer, was a staunch eighteenth-century Independent, who, until his dying day, steadfastly refused to formally associate with the Church of England. It was his father who had to pay the price for independence, however, having three times been imprisoned. Nevertheless, it was the son, Isaac, who would become "the leading figure among English protestant dissenters."[1]

Privately educated, learning several languages in the process, a local doctor took notice of Isaac's intellectual gifts and offered to send him to university, but he refused, knowing that such a commitment would require conformity to the state church. After studying in a small dissenting academy in N. E. London, Watts began to tutor, and preached his first sermon on his twenty-fourth birthday, July 17, 1698. In 1699 he began his ministry as assistant pastor in a church once served by the noted Puritan divine, John Owen. The same church called him as head pastor in 1702, and he remained in that post the rest of his life.

Although terribly ill, once suffering a breakdown that lasted nearly four years, Watts continued his productivity, corresponding widely, and developing a life-long friendship with Philip Doddridge, who would later co-edit Watt's life works. It is as a hymn writer and poet, however, where Watts gained his fame. His hymns were so many, they were collected together in a book made up of three parts: biblical texts, general divine subjects, and hymns for the Lord's Supper. His quill scarcely rested, however, as he also wrote a catechism and several educational books. It is in the last genre, in fact, where a Doddridge biographer suggests Watts shone brightest. "His best work," writes Malcolm Deacon, "is *The Improvement of the Mind*."[2] What is best is a matter of subjective opinion; it is certainly true, on the other hand, that "it was as poet and hymn writer that Watts made his most lasting impact."[3]

1. Isabel Rivers, "Watts, Isaac (1674–1748)," in *Oxford Dictionary of National Biography*, ed. H. C. G. Matthew and Brian Harrison (Oxford: OUP, 2004), http://www.oxforddnb.com/view/article/28888 (accessed August 12, 2008).

2. Malcolm Deacon, *Philip Doddridge of Northampton*, (Northampton: Northamptonshire Libraries, 1980), 151.

3. Rivers.

His 1731 work, *An Humble Attempt Towards the Revival of Practical Religion Among Christians By a Serious Address to Ministers and People in Some Occasional Discourses*, is his contribution to the concern for the state of English clergy. Clearly, the subject of his concern is the state of nonconforming clergy, of which he clearly identifies himself.[4] Originally published as an ordination sermon for a friend, someone decided it needed a wider audience. In the work, Watts develops his advice around four warnings. First, the minister must take heed to his (or her) personal religion. Second, one must take heed to one's public studies and preparations. Third, a minister must take heed to his (or her) public labors. Finally, the careful minister will give attention to conversation.

Watts lived at a time that overlapped the remarkable ministries of both Bull and Burnet, yet he came from a completely different ecclesiastical perspective. He steadfastly refused to join the state church, much less sign any oath to any king. His ecclesiastical and political convictions were at radical odds with both Bull and Burnet; yet, as we will see, the gist of his *Humble Attempt* bears a striking resemblance to both.

JOHN MASON

Like Watts, Mason was an independent minister. Born in Dunmow, Essex in 1706, the younger Mason was also the product of an Independent father (also John Mason), and grandson of the millenarian and hymn writer of the same name. In the 1720s, Mason entered ministry as tutor to the family of John Feaskes, and followed in 1729 as pastor of West Street Independent Chapel in Surrey. In 1746, Mason followed John Oakes as minister of Crossbrook, Cheshunt, Hertfordshire, where he remained until his death in 1763.

Probably Mason's greatest work was his 1745 *Treatise on Self-Knowledge*, which was popular into the next century. By 1835, his treatise had gone through twenty editions and been translated into several languages.[5] It was a work "esteemed by able and impartial judges, as one of the most useful treatises on practical piety that was ever written in

---

4. Isaac Watts, *An Humble Attempt Towards the Revival of Practical Religion Among Christians By a Serious Address to Ministers and People in Some Occasional Discourses*, (1742), 77.

5. Alan Ruston, "Mason, John (1706–1763)," in *Oxford Dictionary of National Biography*, ed. H. C. G. Matthew and Brian Harrison (Oxford: OUP, 2004), http://www.oxforddnb.com/view/article/18283 (accessed August 12, 2008).

English, or perhaps in any language."[6] The *Treatise* is a three part exposition on why self-knowledge is so important and what is required to obtain it. The first section focuses on the nature and importance of studying for self-knowledge. The second extols the excellency of the pursuit and the advantages that come from self-knowledge. Third, he carefully explains how to get such knowledge. Mason's *Treatise* is a bit different than all of the literature presently under consideration, for it is not expressly addressed to clergy; its appeal is broad. As a result, it is so vast in scope that it will guide us in our section on self-knowledge.

A second work by Mason was penned at Cheshunt while he was giving much attention to training young men for ministry. The heart of this work was captured in *The Student and Pastor* (1755).[7] *The Student and Pastor* is an eminently practical and briefer work, but broader in topic than the *Treatise*. There are five main issues the student for ministry must attend to, according to Mason. First is simply good time management. Second, the student must obtain the right method of reading. Third, one must develop good patterns of study, followed, fourth, by a proper way of collecting notes from readings. Finally, the student must create a way of improving his or her thoughts when alone.

The Student and Pastor reveals a wholly different motivation for writing than the others we have encountered so far. Apparently, Mason is neither compelled by a political dynamic nor an overwhelming conviction to write toward the improvement of the *present* state of the clergy. Instead, he writes to intervene early in independent ministerial students' lives to enable them to develop productive lifelong habits. It certainly could be that he decided to put his energy into those starting out in ministry in response to the present state of the clergy, but that is a matter of speculation. Either way, Mason presents us with material that is slightly different than others in both its motivation and its original intended audience.

HENRY OWEN

Biographical information on Henry Owen is a little less accessible than is the case with most of our other writers, although his was clearly a brilliant mind. Born in 1716 and educated at Jesus College, Oxford, Owen

---

6. J. M. Good, 'Memoir', in J. Mason, *Self-knowledge, a Treatise*, 14th ed. (1802), 5–28, quoted in Ruston.

7. John Mason, *The Student and Pastor and An Essay on Elocution*, (1807).

showed a prodigious appetite for formal schooling, earning his BA, MA, MB, and MD. Ordained in 1746, it was his original intention to join the two related professions of ministry and medicine, which he did for the first three years of his ministry. In fact, it appears that the only reason he quit practicing medicine was due to his own health concerns. Not unlike others of his day, Owen held two livings simultaneously, one at St. Olave's in London, and the other at Edmonton, Middlesex.

His first published work was on mathematics; later he focused great attention on biblical criticism, and then produced a few new editions of classical Greek works. Later yet, he joined in defending the truth of Christianity through both miracles and prophecies fulfilled. His *Directions for Young Students in Divinity* appeared in 1766. Unique among others, Owen identifies himself as an elder pastor, and makes it clear from the outset that his real intention is to assist those without the advantage of university education.[8] Built upon Paul's notion in 1 Timothy 3.1 that the office of elder is a high calling, he concludes, "The more highly they think of the office, the more care they will employ informing themselves to it."[9] His argument revolves around two qualifications he deems necessary for ministry: holiness, which is most important, and literary accomplishments.

As only a physician and minister could really say, Owen believes the latter profession is "far superior to all other professions, as the soul is superior to the body. For other professions, relate only to the concerns of the body for the short term of its mortal state; whereas this is employed in promoting the welfare and happiness of the soul through the endless ages of eternity."[10] Where Owen stood on issues of ecclesiastical and political debate is not easily known, but his work presents another unique contribution to the issue of how ministers can develop the habits necessary to shield them from the hazards incumbent to their profession.

HENRY HANDLEY NORRIS

The final contributor to our inquiry is the latest born, 1771. After taking the BA and MA from Pembroke College, Cambridge, Henry Norris was ordained in 1796 and installed as curate at Hackney. A key feature of Norris' biography is his remarkable wealth from an inheritance that

8. Henry Owen, *Directions for Young Students in Divinity*, (1810), v.
9. Ibid., 13.
10. Ibid., 11–12.

enabled him to endow a chapel at Hackney, where he continued to serve until his death in 1850. In the process, he also financed the establishment of two schools, one for boys and the other for girls.

Described as a "Pre-Tractarian Tory high-churchman,"[11] his wealth afforded him great power. In fact, Norris became known as "bishop maker" because as a formality, every bishopric that came open was offered to him, which he courteously refused, which prompted the archbishop to ask him for a recommendation. Norris' political and ecclesiastical persuasion can be seen after he purchased the *British Critic* periodical in 1811 and used it to castigate evangelicals and dissenters, whom he saw as a serious threat to the church, just as the Puritans were to Charles I. Indeed, "Norris' high-churchmanship was characterized by a rigidity and narrowly anti-evangelical animus."[12] He joined in efforts to tighten the use of the *Book of Common Prayer*, wanted greater decorum and ceremony in public worship, and had a high ideal of church uniformity. It is fitting then, that in his *Manual for the Parish Priest* (1815), he makes careful mention of the importance of clerical garb.[13]

His *Manual* shows dependence upon Burnet, and like Bull, clearly emerges out of a concern over church dissenters and nonconformists. It is these groups from which Anglican clergy must guard their flocks. "The spirit of proselytism rages to such a degree amongst some bodies of dissenters that the hard work of pastors cannot prevent even the well-inclined part of his flock being seduced from the doctrine and discipline of the Church."[14]

Norris goes on to tout the glories of the Church of England, noting that "the order of prayer prescribed by the Church of England, is itself a body of divinity. In it, all the doctrines, all the leading principles, and all the precepts of our religion are summed up." Clearly, Norris writes with a pro-Anglican, anti-dissenter motivation, but once again, his work bears a striking similarity to the others in its basic thrust. Not uncommon in

---

11. Peter B. Nockles, "Norris, Henry Handley (1771–1850)," in *Oxford Dictionary of National Biography*, ed. H. C. G. Matthew and Brian Harrison (Oxford: OUP, 2004); online ed., ed. Lawrence Goldman, May 2007, http://www.oxforddnb.com/view/article/20274 (accessed August 12, 2008).

12. Ibid.

13. Henry Handley Norris, *A Manual for the Parish Priest, Being a Few Hints on the Pastoral Care to the Younger Clergy of the Church of England*, (1815), 7.

14. Ibid., 4.

this genre of pastoral literature, Norris is sure to end with a dire warning: "And if it shall happen the same Church, or any member thereof, do take any hurt or hindrance, by reason of your negligence, you know the greatness of the fault, and also the horrible punishment that will ensue."

It is these several writers who composed much of the material that forms the basis of the advice to pastors we will now examine. We have seen the significant differences in political and ecclesiastical conviction among them, which will later help us appreciate the commonness shared in their actual advice. This advice will be categorized into three areas, although we must not be guilty of ignoring the fact that there are many other pieces of advice found scattered throughout their writings that make reading through them a valuable exercise. This categorization is built upon a desire to identify the most common pieces of advice among them. Again, we note that there is tremendous unity in the essential advice they offer pastors to protect themselves from the hazards that come by virtue of serving in professional ministry.

Chapter 11

Retirement

The bow will not bear to always be bent.

It is certainly legitimate to distinguish between retirement and solitude, for one can rest from work, yet remain surrounded by people. Conversely, one can withdraw into solitude, yet persist in activity. Occasionally the English pastoral theologians make this distinction, but usually they link the two; so in their thinking, typically a pastor retires to solitude or enters into solitude for the purpose of retiring.

However they work out the details, there seems to be uniform agreement among these writers that essential to healthy ministry is regular withdrawal, unaccompanied, from the routines of ministry. To Henry Norris, this solitude is so important that it must not be entered into lightly, for the pastor must "be able, comfortably to pass a series of days without society."[1] To these writers, retirement is not a one or two hour detour from regular work; effective retirement lasts days, not hours. Again, their stress on this activity makes it apparent that to these pastoral writers, retirement into solitude was a non-negotiable. Paley suggested that it is "the foundation of almost all other good habits."[2] He immediately follows with a serious demand: "Learn to live alone."[3] The fact is, Paley insists, "Half of your

---

1. Henry Handley Norris, *A Manual for the Parish Priest, Being a Few Hints on the Pastoral Care to the Younger Clergy of the Church of England*, (1815), 20.

2. William Paley, *Rules and Advice to the Clergy of the Dicese of Down and Conner* (1663), 14.

3. Ibid.

faults originate from the want of this faculty."[4] Herein lay the connection between the hazards these authors warn about, and the advice they offer: A failure to practice these habits exposes one to the spiritual hazards inherent in ministry. Norris explains, "The bow will not bear to always be bent."[5] Out of this awareness comes the advice to regularly retire.

Why is solitary withdrawal so critical in their thinking? John Mason offers a succinct answer: "The great advantage of being alone is, that you may chuse [sic] your company; either your books, your friends, your God, or yourself."[6] The benefit of withdrawing is that one gains the gift of choosing influences; whereas, in the regular routine of pastoral ministry, there is little control over what input comes. So the writers might speak of being strengthened by withdrawal, resulting in their increased ability to resist temptation. Retiring for a period of time offers one the advantage of being free to concentrate on the influences the pastor desires in order to help him or her seek self-improvement.

What these writers suggest should be done during these periods of withdrawal demonstrates that complete retirement is not usually in order. The pastoral advice on this subject becomes extremely practical, and often reveals the distinction between retirement and solitude. In solitude, for instance, Paley suggests investing the time in reading and composing sermons. Clearly then, to these writers, withdrawing does not always mean ceasing activity; one might go into solitude for the purpose of actually accomplishing something. Another perspective is offered by Norris, who, due to the danger of the "bow always being bent", advises taking the time away to do something entirely different than ministerial work.[7] He refers to these activities as "amusements" and "relaxations" that are "allowable for the clergy."[8] Of course, coupled with this encouragement comes the warning to make sure that such activity is truly innocent and does not discredit the pastor in the eyes of the church. So Norris introduces recreation as a valid form of retirement, which may modify the concept of retirement always being a solitary activity to possibly being a corporate one.

---

4. Ibid.
5. Norris, 8.
6. John Mason, *The Student and Pastor and An Essay on Elocution*, (1807), 31.
7. Norris, 10.
8. Ibid., 9.

It is somewhat common for the writers to encourage pastors to take this occasion to review their own conduct, including their use of time and their behavior, thoughts, and attitudes during the day. During this time, the pastor might reflect on the minister's call to great piety and virtue, to probity and innocence of manners, meekness and gentleness, humility and self-denial, just contempt of the world, and proper concern for heavenly things.[9] It is imperative, Henry Owen believes, that the pastor be conformed all the way through himself with the very holy demands he preaches to others. Another stark reality that demands this self-reflective practice is rooted in the oft' repeated warning that the Lord himself "will require these souls at his hands . . . ."[10]

Mason devotes all of chapter 5 to the importance of solitude in retirement, and titles the chapter, "Concerning the Improvement of Our Thoughts When Alone."[11] It is a practice, he argues, that includes meditation on Scripture and reviewing things said or even heard. Interestingly, and uniquely, Mason also enjoins his readers to always be on the watch, however, for the intrusion of the devil.[12] He completes his thoughts by advising the pastor concerning what to do in this time alone with God. It must be a time to earnestly implore his help and contemplate the reality of his presence with them.

In summary, James Bradley is helpful when he suggests that these writers urge the clergy to practice being alone for three reasons.[13] First, it affords the minister the opportunity to gain a deeper knowledge of God, in that it allows one the time necessary to contemplate the things of God. Second, it gives clergy the opportunity to make plans for service, such as Paley suggested. Finally, it presents people with the unique opportunity to pursue the important quest for self-knowledge.

---

9. Henry Owen, *Directions for Young Students in Divinity*, (1810), 17–18.

10. Ibid., 21.

11. Mason, 30.

12. Ibid., 31.

13. James Bradley, "Solitude, Self-Knowledge, and the Disciplines of Self-Control," (unpublished manuscript, Fuller Theological Seminary), 1–2.

Chapter 12

Self-Knowledge

Make self-knowledge the great study, and self-government the great business, of your life.

A CHIEF AIM IN withdrawing into solitude is to seek a greater knowledge of one's self. Naturally, John Mason's *Treatise on Self-Knowledge* provides guidance on the subject. Although not written specifically to clergy, Mason was a pastoral writer of this period, and his *Treatise* was recognized and recommended by other pastoral writers.[1] Here, Mason argues that students will find no pursuit more necessary, aside from the study of Scripture itself, than knowing oneself. "Would you live and act consistently, either as a man or a Christian, you must know yourself . . . make self-knowledge the great study, and self-government the great business, of your life."[2] Self-knowledge is so significant that to it "every branch of human literature is subordinate, and ought to be subservient."[3] After showing the precedence in Scripture for knowing oneself, Mason then offers a definition: "Self-knowledge is that acquaintance with ourselves, which shows us what we are, and do, and ought to be, and do, in order to our living comfortably and usefully here, and happily hereafter."[4] Furthermore, knowing oneself leads to knowing God.

---

1. See Henry Owen, *Directions for Young Students in Divinity*, (1810), 27.
2. John Mason, *A Treatise on Self-knowledge*, (1802), 253.
3. Mason, x.
4. Ibid., 8.

What is it that one looks for when regarding the self? Again, selections from Mason's very thorough *Treatise* will serve as a template. First, self-knowledge is important for identifying one's own talents and capacities. It is extremely important that each parson know his or her strengths and how they individually fit into the whole. According to Mason, a wise person will not seek talents he or she does not have, but will cultivate the ones he possesses; in fact, taking a lead from 1 Timothy 4.14, he points out that each must stir up the gift that is within. Without a careful observation of what one's talents are, he (or she) might "sink under the weight he lays upon himself."[5] Another writer, John Erskine, makes a pointed comment in this regard: "A minister should study himself. He should not only be acquainted with his own spiritual state, but with the particular turn of his genius: for, God having distributed among ministers various gifts, and thereby fitted them to answer different purposes in his service, our usefulness will in a great measure depend upon knowing what our gift is."[6]

A second facet of self-knowledge that makes its pursuit so necessary is that it enables one to gain knowledge of one's constitutional sins.[7] "Constitutional sins" is a label for the sins of the heart, those sins that are imbedded in one's character. Watching one's outward behavior provides a clear indication of the sins of the heart. Indeed, the sins of the heart are criminal in comparison to outward actions, so the one "engaged in the study of himself, must be content to know the worst of himself."[8] Like Moses, Mason warns, you stick your hand in your bosom and it might come out as leprous as snow.

Self-knowledge, third, affords one an awareness of the temptations most dangerous to his or her own person.[9] Knowing the self not only affords one the knowledge of his or her own genius, but grants a person insight into where their greatest weaknesses lay. Self-knowledge allows a person to know when she or he is in the greatest danger of transgressing, so it provides a call to watchfulness. So, fourth, it gives people an awareness of their natural tempers, which speaks of their own disposition and

---

5. Ibid., 44.

6. John Erskine, "Qualifications Necessary for Teachers of Christianity," in *Doctrinal and Occasional Sermons*, (1750), 30.

7. Mason, *Treatise*, 50.

8. Ibid., 54.

9. Ibid., 56.

passion.[10] Since people think in completely different ways, time spent in self-knowledge will yield such awareness; in fact, it will produce knowledge of what lies in the secret springs of one's actions. Good self-knowledge, in other words, allows a person to know what truly motivates him or her. To shy away from the invitation to self-knowledge will inevitably lead to self-deception, a great danger pastors must beware of.[11]

Fifth, and finally, self-knowledge bears the fruit of learning just how sensitive one is to being manipulated by "applause."[12] Since one of the great hazards of pastoral ministry is pride, and the accolades one might get in ministry can lead to pride, self-knowledge is a key means by which this can be combated. Mason suggests that everyone has an appetite for fame, so each must beware lest he become "willing to sacrifice the esteem of all wise and good men, to the shouts of the giddy multitude."[13]

Interestingly, the benefits one derives from self-study are not just interior insights. For instance, several of the writers note that this habit will afford the practitioner the all-important attribute of self-government. Beyond just knowledge comes discipline, which George Herbert described using British naval imagery: Self-government allows one to be "absolute master and commander of himself."[14] Mason describes this benefit as applying directly to the mind. "Next to the regulation of the appetites and passions, the most important branch of self-government is the command of our thoughts; which, without a strict guard, will be apt to ramble."[15] Norris, who instructs pastors to review their own conduct during times of self-examination, also indicates that such action will result in guidance: "Whoever rigidly adheres to the practice of self-examination, will not, I think, deviate far from the way wherein he should walk."[16] Along the same line, self-knowledge results in the privilege of evaluating one's relationship with God and others. Owen points out that the result of careful self-examination is spiritual and relational. After practicing such, he writes, one will learn "whether he has that

10. Ibid., 76.

11. Ibid., 86.

12. Ibid., 87.

13. Ibid., 89.

14. George Herbert, *The Country Parson, The Temple,* ed. John N. Wall, Jr., *The Classics of Western Spirituality* (New York: Paulist Press, 1981), 56.

15. Mason, *Student and Pastor,* 30.

16. Norris, 25.

warm zeal for the glory of God and the honor of his religion; that tender concern for the welfare of men's souls...."[17]

Finally, our writers offer some practical advice on how one can obtain this self-knowledge. The first is Scripture itself. Knowing Scripture allows one to know oneself because when it is read, the reader "will plainly perceive the disposition of his soul – whether he is yet fitted for so sacred a function."[18] In an eminently practical section, Mason offers a second consideration, which he describes as "frequent and fervent prayer."[19] This, in fact, is the most effective means to self-knowledge because the mind is never in a better frame than when it is engaged in prayer.

17. Owen, 22.
18. Ibid., 30.
19. Mason, *Treatise*, 247.

Chapter 13

Study

Dwell at the springhead. Drink deep at the fountain of eternal truth.

STUDY IS CONNECTED BOTH to retirement and self-knowledge, since it is an action undertaken in the former, and a means to the latter. Neither connection provides its legitimacy, however, since it stands on its own. "Ply your studies," writes Bull, "give yourselves to reading, chiefly the holy Scriptures, and the writings of the learned men that have explained them to you."[1] Norris, mentioning the manners and habits necessary to effective ministry, connects reading to a good redemption of time; in fact, he advises, "Always have a book in hand to fill up the straggling minutes."[2] Study was regarded as so essential, that the highly regarded *Discourse* of Gilbert Burnet regards it as one of two major preparations necessary for ministers; the first being a right temper, and the second, learning.[3]

Not surprisingly, the advice material is filled with instructions to first study the Scriptures; but there are at least two other characteristics of this advice. First, there is consistent advice from the writers to read the Scriptures in the original languages. The thought is based upon the minister's call to properly understand the Scripture, which requires some skill in languages. So Mason urges his students, "Go to the fountain head. Read

---

1. George Bull, "A Visitation Sermon Concerning the Great Difficulties and Danger of the Priestly Office" in *A Companion for the Candidates for Holy Orders* (1794), 53.

2. Henry Handley Norris, *A Manual for the Parish Priest, Being a Few Hints on the Pastoral Care to the Younger Clergy of the Church of England*, 19.

3. Gilbert Burnet, *A Discourse of the Pastoral Care* (1692), 142.

original authors, rather than those who translate or retail [recount] their thoughts. It will give you more satisfaction, more certainty, more judgment, and more confidence . . . ."[4] Burnet is convinced that one cannot be sure about one's own preaching without skill in the original languages. "He cannot have this so sure, unless he understands the Greek so well."[5] In Mason's advice to his students, he offers several guidelines for studying, the first of which is to read a chapter each day in both Hebrew and Greek.[6]

A second bit of advice that is common among these writers is to study broadly. At one level, it comes as no surprise that many of the writers present extensive collections of theological literature as recommendations for learning, along with a specific recommendation of the church fathers. Owen produces several pages of theologically oriented literature he recommends,[7] as does Burnet.[8] But Watts is particularly clear that the subject of clerical study must go beyond the theological, so he devotes much material to describing this literature.[9] Some of the subjects do not appear to be directly relevant to sacred studies. These works, Watts suggests, are to be studied simply for the purpose of developing good reasoning skills. Such subjects as math and geometry might serve to that end.[10] No obscurantist, Watts also promotes the study of science, which he believes helps us honor God. Studying helpful learning methods and good oratory skill is also productive. Without an apparent hint of apology, this dissenter even recommends a good study of some of the heathen authors, apparently understanding that truth is truth no matter its source.[11]

Finally, Mason, in his *Student and Pastor*, offers some very practical advice to pastors on how one should go about the reading task.[12] Such instruction can be summarized as follows: Do not read indiscriminately. Do not read in hopes that the book will get better; since the minister

---

4. John Mason, *The Student and Pastor and An Essay on Elocution*, (1807), 19.

5. Burnet, 165.

6. Mason, 20.

7. Henry Owen, *Directions for Young Students in Divinity*, (1810), 32ff.

8. Burnet, 165ff.

9. Isaac Watts, *An Humble Attempt Towards the Revival of Practical Religion Among Christians By a Serious Address to Ministers and People in Some Occasional Discourses*, (1742), 12ff.

10. Ibid., 12.

11. Ibid., 15.

12. See Mason, *Student and Pastor*, c2.

has not the time to waste on such exercises, move on to another more productive work. In the process, Mason instructs, take note of certain authors and use them to inform your own writing style. If the pastor reads a well-regarded author, but finds nothing of substance, the pastor needs to realize he or she has probably made the wrong selection. His advice even extends into the very practical: Get a good overview of the book first, and do not be afraid to mark it up! Mason does not stop with this pastoral advice, for he then moves on to give specific instructions as to how to study for a sermon in his third chapter.

Again, it may be prudent to reiterate that all pastoral study begins and ends with Scripture. It is the Scripture that reigns supreme. As Mason writes in a personal letter, "Dwell at the springhead. Drink deep at the fountain of eternal truth."[13]

---

13. John Mason, "Letter to a Friend," in *The Student and Pastor and An Essay on Elocution*, (London: H.D. Symonds, Paternoster, 1807), 181.

Conclusion

Based on three ancient documents, we have identified a common concern for the spiritual dangers priests, or pastors, have to face by virtue of their engagement in ministry. These three documents share a common context in that each writer, in a different time and place, was attempting to explain his initial rejection of the call to office. In each of the three, a paramount concern to protect one's own spiritual life surfaced, based upon the conviction that with pastoral (priestly) ministry, there is an attached exposure to dangerous spiritual realities. The temptations and vexations that come with that ministry are profound; indeed, profound enough to have compelled each of these writers to flee the call. We then noted the clear connection between these three earlier writers and certain English pastoral writers of the seventeenth and eighteenth centuries. Suggesting the latter were to some degree dependent upon the former, we highlighted the same concerns about spiritual hazards even though those concerns surfaced in entirely different circumstances. Whether in the form of treatises or sermons, these English writers, although diverse in theological and political conviction, agree with the sentiment of the earlier three writers by surfacing the same dangers to the spiritual health and vitality of their clergy.

Last, we surveyed the same body of English literature in search of preventative measures, and discovered that several themes were repeated and presented as measures to be taken in order to address the hazards inherent in ministry. It was discovered that retirement with solitude, self-knowledge, and study, were three frequently suggested practices that must characterize a minister's life if there is going to be success in overcoming the hazards sure to be encountered.

Again, we must observe a remarkable similarity of content among the English pastoral writers. Although these Englishmen wrote from different motivations, the thrust of their message is the same from writer to writer. We have noticed that not a few of our authors wrote with the intention of pushing certain religious and political agenda. George Bull seems to write out of a deep concern over the effects of the Toleration Act, and it is certainly that same Act that drives Gilbert Burnet in his *Discourse*, although his opinion of the Act differed. Certainly, a resentment of dissenters drives Henry Norris, while Issac Watts, John Mason (themselves dissenters), and William Paley seem to write out of a sheer concern for the state of contemporary clergy. Nevertheless, we notice a great similarity in the final products of these writers. So, if we remove the slights aimed at those of differing convictions, the overlap of material here is remarkable. Despite the mixed motives, they all share a concern for the state of the clergy. James Bradley agrees: "The most noteworthy characteristic of the English tradition of practical theology is its theological coherence. From 1650 to 1850, a comparison of the authors of pastoral theology and the letters of advice to young ministers in a wide variety of denominations failed to reveal significant theological discrepancies between them. Differences of taste and conflicting estimates of the worth of certain writers persisted, but the commonality of the desired goal for the prospective minister is convincingly shown...."[1]

Cornwall notes the same unity, and after offering specific examples, states, "Herbert, Baxter, Taylor, [John] Bunyan, and [William] Bates all shared the same anxieties about the state of the church."[2] They each call ministers to faithfulness and high ideals. They all urge their ministers to be learned in Scripture and broad study, to be pious, respectable, humble, and faithful to their call. Even in the details, there is remarkable similarity that reveals some level of dependence upon one another. Indeed, Mason, the Independent, quotes Burnet, the Anglican faithful.[3] Norris does the same, and Henry Owen even published an abridgment of Burnet.[4] In fact,

---

1. James Bradley, "The Nineteenth Century," in *Theological Education in the Evangelical Tradition*, eds. D.G. Hart and R. Albert Mohler, Jr. (Grand Rapids: Baker Book House, 1996), 150.

2. Robert Cornwall, *Gilbert Burnet's Discourse of the Pastoral Care* (Lewiston: Edwin Mellen Press, 1997), 34.

3. John Mason, *Student and Pastor*, (1807), 122.

4. Henry Handley Norris, *A Manual for the Parish Priest, Being a Few Hints on the Pastoral Care to the Younger Clergy of the Church of England*, (1815), 5. On Owen, see Bradley, 150.

as has already been noted, Burnet is himself indebted to Baxter, as are both Mason and Watts.[5] Cornwall notices the same overlap while reflecting on Burnet, the subject of his work: "As one examines Burnet's treatise, he or she will see that Burnet shared many areas of concern with other writers on the theme of pastoral theology, whether they were Nonconformists, high churchmen, or low churchmen."[6] Owen, who shows no apparent affinity with Independents, nevertheless, recommends Mason's *Treatise*.[7] No matter the precise motivation, intended audience, or theological and political conviction, the advice offered blends together, to the degree that if one were to read them in ignorance of their authors' personal differences, most readers would probably not notice there are any differences.

Based on this reality, one cannot help but notice a sense of timelessness in their concerns and advice. Put another way, the sometimes significant differences between our writer's motivations, convictions, and intentions, makes the unity of their advice transcend the confines of their era. In some sense then, they beg to be considered as applicable to our own day. This, of course, leads us to a practical question: If their advice is timeless, why don't we talk about the same spiritual hazards today? Out of the plethora of contemporary books being published, where is a similar concern expressed with the same passion? To conclude, I will offer two possible answers.

A HIGHER VIEW OF THE MINISTRY

In the first place, our writers show a greater concern over the spiritual hazards of ministry because their view of the ministry itself was generally much higher than our own. With the plethora of pastoral ministry books coming off the press from publishers around the world, there is no shortage of metaphors and images for this most unique line of work. For instance, Howard Rice has reduced the images to four, which he bases on "the growing literacy of parishioners [which] has meant change for the pastor's role."[8] First, Rice refers to the contemporary model of the pastor as educator. Even though the role of biblical educator is ancient, the model of the professional educator who offers biblical literacy is recent.

---

5. Gilbert Burnet, *A Discourse of the Pastoral Care* (1692), 29. On Mason and Watts, see Bradley, 149.

6.. Cornwall, 34.

7. Henry Owen, *Directions for Young Students in Divinity*, (1810), 27.

8. Howard Rice, *The Pastor as Spiritual Guide* (Nashville: Upper Room, 1998), 25.

The psychology model, second in Rice's list, reflects the focus of the pastor on the work of counseling. Third is social change, which emphasizes the pastor's work in the great tradition of clergy like Martin Luther King, Jr. Finally, a more recent addition to the images of pastoral ministry is the pastor as business manager, where the study has been replaced with the office. Rice, however, goes on to suggest his own image, which is broader, and incorporates aspects of all four. Rice's suggestion is the older image of the pastor as spiritual guide, closely connected to the notion of the pastor as cure of souls.[9]

Reflecting an idea that is rooted in the Reformation, others prefer the image of the pastor as minister of the Word. John Stott plainly states that the pastoral ministry "was and is a ministry of the Word . . . for the chief responsibility of the pastor who 'tends' his sheep is to 'feed' them."[10] The vision that Stott purports is very much a ministry that revolves around Scripture; indeed, everything the pastor does is an expression of this idea.[11] Jay Adams essentially suggests the same: "Practical ministry can never be anything less than the ministry of the Word."[12]

More recently a stress has been placed on the pastor as the one who advertises and markets the work of the local church, no doubt due to the secularization of society and the loss of an America where "everyone goes to church." H. B. London, a respected leader among evangelical pastors, acknowledges and affirms, this trend. "Nearly every pastor is a salesman or a marketer of one kind or another because . . . we have a philosophy to sell . . . The best marketers and best salesmen will have more converts, will have more people, will take home more money . . . Evangelicals are marketers because they're really passionate about their product."[13]

Such a hodge-podge of images for the pastor has the potential of leaving one in complete confusion, resulting in a lack of coherence among the many ministerial tasks. So Eugene Peterson, an author who repeatedly sounds the alarm over the contemporary approach to pastoral ministry,

---

9. Ibid., 34ff.

10. John R. W. Stott, *Between Two Worlds: The Art of Preaching in the Twentieth Century* (Grand Rapids: William B. Eerdmans Co., 1982), 118.

11. Ibid., 120.

12. Jay E. Adams, *Shepherding God's Flock* (Grand Rapids: Zondervan, 1975), 2.

13. G. Jeffrey MacDonald, "Churches Seeking Marketing-Savvy Breed of Pastor," *The Christian Science Monitor*, August 19, 2005. http://www.csmonitor.com/2005/0819/p01s03-ussc.html (accessed August 19, 2005).

expresses grave concern: "The pastors of America have metamorphosed into a company of shopkeepers, and the shops they keep are churches. They are preoccupied with shopkeeper's concerns—how to keep the customers happy, how to lure customers away from competitors down the street, how to package the goods so that the customers will lay out more money."[14] Quite frankly, Peterson charges, "They have gone whoring after other gods."[15]

While certainly not every contemporary pastor has a shallow or narrow understanding of the pastorate, and not everything written about the role minimizes it, the writers we have been considering consistently describe an exalted and glorious ministry that makes the aforementioned images seem terribly narrow and disappointingly shallow. As we have seen, Gregory of Nazianzus' statement represents the quintessence of this attitude: "But the scope of our art is to provide the soul with wings, to rescue it from the world and give it to God, and to watch over that which is in His image, if it abides, to take it by the hand, if it is in danger, to restore it, if ruined, to make Christ to dwell in the heart by the Spirit: and, in short, to deify, and bestow heavenly bliss upon, one who belongs to the heavenly host."[16] Indeed, Gregory states, "The guiding of man, the most variable and manifold of creatures, seems to me in very deed to be the art of arts and science of sciences."[17] The work of ministry is greater than that of the physician, for the physician's work is limited to the human body, made up of flesh and blood. One wonders, what would Gregory have said of the comparison of the pastor to the educator, the psychologist, the social activist, the business manager, and the marketing agent? We have seen Chrysostom's lofty description and his challenge that the pastor is to train the church to "perfect health and incredible beauty."[18] Years later, Burnet echoes the same high calling: "He is to watch over their souls, to keep them from error, and to alarm them out of their sins, by giving them warning of the judgments of God; to visit the sick, and to prepare them for the judgment and the life to come."[19]

14. Eugene Peterson, *Working the Angles* (Grand Rapids: William B. Eerdmans, 1987), 2.
15. Ibid., 1.
16. Gregory of Nazianzus, *Apologeticus de Fuga* (A. D. 362?), 2.23.
17. Gregory the Great, *The Book of Pastoral Rule* (A. D. 590), 2.16.
18. John Chrysostom, *de Sacerdotio* (A. D. 391), 4.2. Further references are in-text.
19. Gilbert Burnet, 3.

One can begin to speculate on the reasons these writers' vision of pastoral ministry was so exalted. Instead of being restrained by a narrow conception of the task as something like human social work, these writers saw their labor as rescuing a soul from the world to "give it to God." Instead of viewing themselves as psychologists probing for root causes, these thinkers envisioned themselves as making "Christ to dwell in the heart by the Spirit." Instead of perceiving their work as inculcating information into people, they saw themselves training people to "perfect health and incredible beauty." We are reminded of Henry Owen's conviction: "The more highly they think of the office, the more care they will employ informing themselves to it."[20] In short, they understood their work to be addressed to the deepest core of the human person, a task carrying eternal implications.

No doubt, this awareness also fueled their understanding of the awfulness of their task. All of their writings are connected by a profound awareness of the responsibility they bore for the souls of their people. This was not simply an antiquated fourth-century idea; Burnet echoes the same concern. Pastors "ought to consider themselves under very strict obligations, by that charge of which they must give a severe account at the great day, in which the blood of all those who perished through their neglect and default, shall be required at their hands."[21] It is little wonder that our first three writers fled from the call, intimidated by the responsibility incumbent upon them to return to God a pure people. Similarly, the English pastoral theologians reflect a deep awareness as they implore their pastoral listeners and hearers to take heed to themselves. Were such a perception of ministry held today, one cannot help but wonder if the same vehement warnings and exhortation would return to our lips and pens.

A PROFOUND VIEW OF SIN

A second reason why contemporary pastoral literature does not reflect the same kind of profound spiritual warning is that the earlier writers had a deeper and more profound view of sin. E. Brooks Holifield has traced the gradual movement in pastoral theology from the concept of curing the sin-sick soul to enhancing one's self-perception.[22] He begins his work

---

20. Henry Owen, *Directions for Young Students in Divinity*, (1810), 13.
21. Ibid., 28–29.
22. E. Brooks Holifield, *A History of Pastoral Care in America: From Salvation to Self-*

by tracking differing conceptions of sin through various Christian traditions, beginning with the Roman Catholic stress on the inherited condition and discrete acts.[23] The Lutheran stress was upon the incapacity of the individual to trust God,[24] while the Anglican focused on gradual growth that would become known as moralism, which grew to include a "willful breaching of civil peace and religious unity."[25] To Holifield, the Anglican perspective was a notion of disorder that required the clergy to assure proper order in the lives of their parishioners. Fourth, the Reformed tradition, while affirming the Lutheran notion of unfaithfulness, tended to focus upon disobedience and idolatry, with the resultant Puritan movement placing heavy stress on the latter.[26] Beyond these four great strands of Christian tradition, America saw a tremendously influential activist piety emerge in the nineteenth century that viewed sin as a specific act of transgression, a voluntary act of the will.[27] With the influence of Sigmund Freud, sin was understood as something deep in the inner person; in particular, sin was understood as false pride.[28] Finally, in twentieth-century America, sin was understood in terms of self-realization, personal development, and growth.[29]

Against the present backdrop of pop-psychology, where sin is understood as self-offense, one can see that the writers under our consideration had a more profound understanding of sin and an attendant greater horror of it. However these writers might have defined sin had they attempted a precise theological expression, they clearly saw it as deeper, more pervasive, more potent, and more destructive than it is often perceived today. Significantly, the greatest emphasis of our writers is not upon sin's outward acts, but the deep inward stain that is sin. Their concerns are over sins that hide in the recesses of the heart, such as pride, ambition, and seeking applause. Scarcely is there mention made of the more outward sins of the sexual variety that are so often the focus of contemporary attention. Contrary to understanding sin as an affront against the self,

Realization (Nashville: Abingdon, 1983).

23. Ibid., 18.
24. Ibid., 19.
25. Ibid., 21.
26. Ibid., 22.
27. Ibid., 352.
28. Ibid.
29. Ibid.

these writers tended to see it as an affront against God stemming from our natural self-orientation. It is precisely this deep and abiding tendency toward self-service that was seen to undermine God-honoring pastoral work. While we must acknowledge the fact that each of our writers may have articulated a theology of sin slightly different from one another, it remains true that they shared a unified terror of its presence in the heart and a repellant fear of its potential to lure the churches' shepherds onto the path of destruction, leading to the downfall of many.

Chrysostom, for one, clearly believed that sin defiles and contaminates the inner person, a thing so intense that it comes against the soul and spawns unspeakable mayhem.[30] Sin is that mysterious power that will kill enthusiasm and paralyze spiritual energy, two essential ingredients for carrying out priestly ministry. Indeed, it is so serious that one must "live like disembodied spirits who are not hounded by envy or vainglory" (5.8). In a warning that impinges on the nerve of contemporary understandings of sin, Chrysostom warns that popular esteem is an "elusive, invisible, savage monster" (5.8). Even more than a thousand years later, Richard Baxter carries the same weighty view. Sin is not merely an act that results in temporal discomfort; it is the pervasive power that brings glory to Satan in his rebellion against Jesus.[31] In this cosmic framework, the pastor who falls prey does "much service to him that was your enemy."[32] To be sure, sin can express itself as an identifiable act, even an act of the heart, and its danger is that one sin will incline the person toward another, for while it may lie dormant, it will be revived by the slightest spark.[33]

It comes as no surprise that the alarm over sin that flows from the pens of these writers contain great warnings, not just about the personal implications of sin, but the fallout it causes in the lives of those nearby. So Gregory the Great: "Wherefore it is necessary that they guard themselves so much the more cautiously from sin as by the bad things they do they die not alone, *but are guilty of the souls of others*, which by their bad example they have destroyed."[34] Baxter adds: "What speedier way is there for the depraving and undoing of the people, than the depravity of their

---

30. John Chrysostom, *De Sacerdotio* (AD 391), 6.11.

31. Richard Baxter, *The Reformed Pastor* (Edinburgh: The Banner of Truth Trust, 2005), 75.

32. Ibid.

33. Ibid., 73.

34. Gregory the Great, *The Book of Pastoral Rule* (AD 590), 3.4. Italics, mine.

guides?"[35] Clearly, these writers did not view sin as an offense limited to the arena of self-harm.

Thus, the voices of the writers we have considered are voices that deserve to be heard again. Amid the diversity of time, theological conviction, place, and political intrigue, there is an amazingly unified concern expressed. What is more, this unity in the midst of diversity gives the warnings themselves a sense of timelessness and heightens their urgency. Frequent mention of pride, ambition, neglect of the self, the influential opinion of others, and the eventual judgment the minister faces, are clearly issues that span time, culture, and theological particularities. Are not the warnings the same today despite our fixation on outward sins and our tendency to relegate their impact to the realm of self-esteem? Do not Paley's six concerns about what can happen to the pastor as his or her duty is performed speak just as loudly in the twenty-first century as in the eighteenth?

Finally, if the concerns remain the same, then so must the solutions. If, in the thinking of the English pastoral theologians, the remedy included retirement, self-knowledge, and study, these must still be the answer. Modern pastors and priests would do well to observe the hazards repeated by these writers, and would be the wiser for incorporating the safeguards into the rhythm of their busy ministerial lives. If today's pastors would give renewed attention to these old documents, there may be a renewal among the clergy that flows over into a renewal among their people.

---

35. Baxter, 39.

Bibliography

Allison, C. Fitzsimons. *The Rise of Moralism: The Proclamation of the Gospel from Hooker to Baxter*. Vancouver: Regent College Publishing, 2003.
Baxter, Richard. *The Autobiography of Richard Baxter*. Everyman's Library. Edited by Ernest Rhys. London: J. M. Dent and Sons, 1931.
Baxter, Richard. *The Reformed Pastor*. Edinburgh: The Banner of Truth Trust, 2005.
Black, J. William. *Reformation Pastors: Richard Baxter and the Ideal of the Reformed Pastor*. Carlisle: Paternoster Press, 2004.
Bradley, James. "Solitude, Self-Knowledge, and the Disciplines of Self-Control." Unpublished manuscript, Fuller Theological Seminary.
———. "The Institutions and Literature of Formation." Lecture, Fuller Theological Seminary, Malibu, CA, October 15, 2007.
———. "The Nineteenth Century." In *Theological Education in the Evangelical Tradition*, edited by D. G. Hart and R. Albert Mohler, Jr., 148–70. Grand Rapids: Baker Book House, 1996.
Bremer, Francis. *Shaping New Englands: Puritan Clergymen in Seventeenth-Century England and New England*. Twayne's United States Author Series. Edited by Pattie Cowell. New York: Twayne Publishers, 1994.
Bull, George. *A Companion for the Candidates for Holy Orders*. Durham: L. Pennington, 1794.
Burnet, Gilbert. *A Discourse of the Pastoral Care*. London: Rose and Crown, 1692.
———. *Gilbert Burnet's Discourse of the Pastoral Care*. Edited by Robert Cornwall. Lewiston: Edwin Mellen Press, 1997.
Burton, Edward, ed. *The Works of George Bull, DD, Lord Bishop of St. Davids*. Oxford: University of Oxford Press, 1846.
Cascoigne, John. *Cambridge in the Age of the Enlightenment*. Cambridge: Cambridge University Press, 1989.
Chadwick, Henry. *The Early Church* New York: Dorset Press, 1986.
Chrysostom, John. *Six Books on the Priesthood*. Translated and edited by Graham Neville. New York: St. Vladimir's Seminary Press, 2002.
Clarke, M. L. *Paley: Evidences for the Man*. Toronto: University of Toronto Press, 1974.
Clarke, T. E. S. and Foxcroft, H. C. *A Life of Gilbert Burnet*. Cambridge: The University Press, 1907.
Cornwall, Robert D. "Bull, George (1634–1710)." In Oxford Dictionary of National Biography, edited by H. C. G. Matthew and Brian Harrison. Oxford: OUP, 2004. http://www.oxforddnb.com/view/article/18283 (accessed August 12, 2008).

Culbertson, Philip L., and Arthur Bradford Shippee, eds. *The Pastor: Readings from the Patristic Period.* Minneapolis: Fortress Press, 1990.
Deacon, Malcolm. *Philip Doddridge of Northampton.* Northampton: Northamptonshire Libraries, 1980.
Douglas, J. D., ed. *The New International Dictionary of the Christian Church.* Grand Rapids: Zondervan Publishing House, 1978.
Eden, Charles Page, ed. *The Whole Works of the Right Reverend Jeremy Taylor, D. D.* 10 vols. London: Longman, Brown, Green, and Longmans, 1854.
Evans, G. R., ed. *A History of Pastoral Care.* London: Cassell, 2000.
Gibson, William. *The Church of England: 1688-1822.* London: Routledge, 2001.
Gonzales, Justo. *The Story of Christianity.* Vol. 1, *The Early Church to the Dawn of the Reformation.* San Francisco: Harper San Francisco, 1984.
Herbert, George. *The Country Parson, The Temple.* Edited by John N. Walls, Jr. The Classics of Western Spirituality. New York: Paulist Press, 1981.
Hole, Robert. *Pulpits, Politics, and Public Order in England: 1760-1832.* Cambridge: University of Cambridge Press, 1989.
Jones, Kirk Byron. *Rest in the Storm: Self-Care Strategies for Clergy and Other Caregivers.* Valley Forge: Judson Press, 2001.
Kant, Immanuel. *Practical Philosophy.* Translated and edited by Mary J. Gregor. Cambridge: Cambridge University Press, 1996.
Kelly, J. N. D. *Golden Mouth.* Grand Rapids: Baker Books, 1995.
Latourette, Kenneth Scott. *A History of Christianity.* New York: Harper and Row Publishers, 1975.
Mason, John. *The Student and Pastor and An Essay on Elocution.* London: H. D. Symonds, Paternoster, 1807.
Nelson, Robert. "The Life of Bishop Bull," in *The Works of George Bull, D. D., Lord Bishop of St. David's,* ed. Rev. Edward Burton, D. D. Oxford: University of Oxford Press, 1846.
Nockles, Peter B. "Norris, Henry Handley (1771-1850)." In Oxford Dictionary of National Biography, edited by H. C. G. Matthew and Brian Harrison. Oxford: OUP, 2004. http://www.oxforddnb.com/view/article/18283 (accessed August 12, 2008).
Norris, Henry Handley. *A Manual for the Parish Priest, Being a Few Hints on the Pastoral Care to the Younger Clergy of the Church of England.* London: F. C. & J. Rivington, 1815.
Oden, Thomas. *Care of Souls in the Classic Tradition.* Philadelphia: Fortress Press, 1984.
Owen, Henry. *Directions for Young Students in Divinity.* F. C. & J. Rivington, London, 1810.
Packer, J. I. *A Quest for Godliness.* Wheaton: Crossway Books, 1990.
Paley, William. *Dangers Incidental to the Clerical Character.* London: R. Faulder, 1795.
Purves, Andrew. *Pastoral Theology in the Classical Tradition.* Louisville: Westminster John Knox Press, 2001.
Quasten, Johannes. *Patrology.* 3 vols. Utrecht: Spectrum Publishers, 1963.
Rivers, Isabel. "Watts, Isaac (1674-1748)." In Oxford Dictionary of National Biography, edited by H. C. G. Matthew and Brian Harrison. Oxford: OUP, 2004. http://www.oxforddnb.com/view/article/18283 (accessed August 12, 2008).
Rosman, Doreen. *The Evolution of the English Churches: 1500-2000.* Cambridge: Cambridge University Press, 2003.

Ruston, Alan. "Mason, John (1706–1763)." In *Oxford Dictionary of National Biography*, edited by H. C. G. Matthew and Brian Harrison. Oxford: OUP, 2004. http://www.oxforddnb.com/view/article/18283 (accessed August 12, 2008).

Spaeth, Donald A. *The Church in the Age of Danger: Parsons and Parishioners 1660–1740*. Cambridge Studies in Early Modern British History. Edited by Anthony Fletcher, John Guy, and John Morrill. Cambridge: Cambridge University Press, 2000.

Spurr, John. *The Post-Reformation Religion, Politics, and Society in Britain: 1603–1714*. New York: Pearson Longman, 2006.

Sterk, Andrea. *Renouncing the World Yet Leading the Church: The Monk-Bishop Is Late Antiquity*. Cambridge: Harvard University Press, 2004.

Taylor, Jeremy. *Rules and Advices to the Clergy of the Diocese of Down and Conner*. London: Richard Royston, 1663. Volz, Carl. *Pastoral Life and Practice in the Early Church*. Minneapolis: Augsburg, 1990.

Wakefield, Gordon S. "Anglican Spirituality." In *Christian Spirituality 3: Post Reformation and Modern*, edited by Louise Dupre and Don E. Saliers, 257–93. New York: Crossroad, 1991.

Walker, Williston. *A History of the Christian Church*. Edinburgh: T. & T. Clark, 1918.

Waterman, A. M. C. "A Cambridge 'Via Media' in Late Georgian Anglicanism." *Journal of Ecclesiastical History* 42, no. 3 (July 1991): 419–36.

Watts, Isaac. *An Humble Attempt Towards the Revival of Practical Religion Among Christians by a Serious Address to Ministers and People in Some Occasional Discourses*. London: James Brackstone, 1742.